Continuing Professional Development

CHANDOS
INFORMATION PROFESSIONAL SERIES

Series Editor: Ruth Rikowski
(email: rikowski@tiscali.co.uk)

Chandos' new series of books are aimed at the busy information professional. They have been specially commissioned to provide the reader with an authoritative view of current thinking. They are designed to provide easy-to-read and (most importantly) practical coverage of topics that are of interest to librarians and other information professionals. If you would like a full listing of current and forthcoming titles, please visit our web site **www.chandospublishing.com** or contact Hannah Grace-Williams on email info@chandospublishing.com or telephone number +44 (0) 1865 884447.

New authors: we are always pleased to receive ideas for new titles; if you would like to write a book for Chandos, please contact Dr Glyn Jones on email gjones@chandospublishing.com or telephone number +44 (0) 1865 884447.

Bulk orders: some organisations buy a number of copies of our books. If you are interested in doing this, we would be pleased to discuss a discount. Please contact Hannah Grace-Williams on email info@chandospublishing.com or telephone number +44 (0) 1865 884447.

Continuing Professional Development

A guide for information professionals

ALAN BRINE

Chandos Publishing
Oxford · England · New Hampshire · USA

Chandos Publishing (Oxford) Limited
Chandos House
5 & 6 Steadys Lane
Stanton Harcourt
Oxford OX29 5RL
UK
Tel: +44 (0) 1865 884447 Fax: +44 (0) 1865 884448
Email: info@chandospublishing.com
www.chandospublishing.com

Chandos Publishing USA
3 Front Street, Suite 331
PO Box 338
Rollinsford, NH 03869
USA
Tel: 603 749 9171 Fax: 603 749 6155
Email: BizBks@aol.com

First published in Great Britain in 2005

ISBN:
1 84334 081 X (paperback)
1 84334 082 8 (hardback)

© A. Brine, 2005

Cover images courtesy of Bytec Solutions Ltd (*www.bytecweb.com*) and David Hibberd (*DAHibberd@aol.com*).

Printed in the UK and USA.

Contents

Acknowledgements

I am grateful to the following for their assistance:

Professor John Feather of Loughborough University for his support and permission to use our joint work here;

The Australian Library and Information Association for permission to use the work they have completed on career development;

The Empathy Project for permission to reproduce their work on mentoring.

Lastly, my utmost thanks to my wife Ann for her untiring proofreading of the text.

List of figures and tables

Figures

Tables

About the author

Alan Brine is Library Systems and IT Manager at De Montfort University library where he runs a team of IT professionals who maintain the library network and associated systems, and also provide support to students. Previously he was Manager for Information Science at the Learning and Teaching Support Network Centre for Information and Computer Sciences at Loughborough University. This was a national centre to support those departments teaching library and information science across the UK, through a mixture of collaborative activities and publications. He has also been Electronic Services Development Manager at the University of Derby and Union Catalogue Project Administrator at Cambridge University Library.

He has a BA (honours) in Library and Information Studies from Ealing College of Higher Education and an MSc in Information Systems and Technology from City University. He is currently studying for a PhD at Loughborough University. He has presented a number of papers on his research at international conferences, including IFLA, many of which have been published in the professional press.

As a chartered member of the Chartered Institute for Library and Information Professionals he is professionally active in its groups, providing training for their members and providing supervision for candidates who are registered for election to become chartered members.

The author may be contacted at:

E-mail: *abrine@dmu.ac.uk*

Introduction

New entrants into the information professions have always needed to obtain practical training beyond their academic study. The broad scope of the academic curriculum is generally agreed and exemplified by agencies in the respective countries, such as the Quality Assurance Agency in the UK, who provide subject benchmarks[1] in defined academic areas. The knowledge and understanding the new professional must acquire is, to some extent, defined. However, less consideration has been given to the skills necessary for the individual to function effectively as an information professional. The acquisition of practical skills is part of the formal educational process; for example, a library and information science (LIS) student will learn how to catalogue, how to search for information and so on. There is, however, less general agreement on the full range of skill-sets, required for effective practice as an information professional.

Allowing for the difference in academic grades when graduates leave their institution with a library and information science degree, they must all acquire the more practical skills associated with the profession. To develop their skills they will be able to apply the theory to their job. This education will continue throughout the individual's working life and will be a combination of acquiring theoretical knowledge and practical skills. Such a development process, throughout one's career, is professional development. To remain effective as a practitioner the library and information professional must ensure their skills remain current.

Planning for development

To ensure the individual develops their skills at appropriate points in their career, or earlier, they must plan. Planning is crucial to ensure that any development measures taken by the individual achieve both the desired outcome expressed by the individual and also some form of progression in their development.

Personal development planning

Personal development planning (PDP) is concerned with enabling students, or other practitioners, to record the development of their skills as they acquire them. It can be argued that personal development is different from professional development, but to the individual it is unlikely to seem different. The individual will wish to develop their skills and progress their career, but planning will take place within their own personal circumstances, even though it is developing them as a library and information professional. The process of PDP is intended to begin the development of the individual at an early stage so that as they develop as a professional the process is familiar.

Skills development cycle

The process of developing skills is similar to that of learning. Kolb[2] describes the 'learning cycle' as having four stages which are cyclical in nature and should all take place to be fully effective. The skills development cycle used by the RAPID Project[3] as exemplified in the skills development cycle

Figure 1.1 Skills development cycle

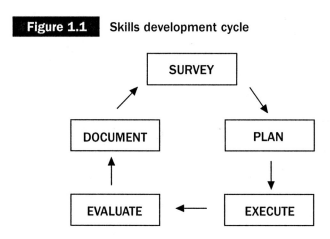

in Figure 1.1 expands the cycle to cater for the development of professional skills.

Individuals should identify the skills they have developed or need to develop through the survey stage. They should review their job role and gather the appropriate evidence to support the skills they have attained, and to what level.

This should be followed by the formation of a plan to obtain the necessary skills required for their development. This plan is then executed. Having carried out their training or development the individual should reflect and evaluate what they have achieved and then document it. They are then ready to begin the cycle again to achieve a higher level of competency. This process complements the analysis of training needs discussed in Chapter 2.

The cycle has been used by other writers to express the same process. Jackson,[4] for example, when discussing the process as a part of personal development planning describes the process as:

- planning;
- doing;
- recording;

- reviewing;

- evaluating.

The first stage looks at how to achieve change, followed by learning by experience and then providing evidence of the experience. He finishes with the individual's reflection on the experience and their judgment on their own development and what more they must undertake.

The reflective practitioner

Reflecting on any activity that one has undertaken is difficult and is an acquired skill. Once it becomes a habit, as it would if a portfolio was constantly being developed and redeveloped, then it becomes second nature to us. Schon[5] describes reflection in two ways. First he describes 'reflection on action', whereby the individual undertakes an activity and then reviews how well it went, whether they achieved what they wanted, and why.

He continues by describing how 'reflection in action' along with professional knowledge, is at the heart of professional practice. The practitioner will reflect on their activities and adjust what they do on a daily basis. This activity is difficult to analyse and even harder to provide evidence for.

A third type of reflection was suggested by Cowan:[6] 'reflection for action' is carried out by the individual so that they can plan future development. These three kinds of reflection will all be performed by the individual during the creation of a portfolio and are the key to creating a successful portfolio. More detail on portfolios can be found in subsequent chapters.

Reflection is therefore exceptionally important to the modern library and information professional. Being able to reflect is a skill that needs to be acquired, since not all individuals are naturally inclined towards a reflective learning style.

Honey and Mumford[7] quote four learning styles that can be adopted by individuals, these being:

- activist;

- reflector;

- theorist;

- pragmatist.

Activists

Those who favour this style will prefer:

- new experiences;
- activities involving teamwork;
- opportunities to lead and present;
- to express ideas outside of formal settings;
- being given difficult tasks to test themselves;
- being involved with other people;
- being able to attempt anything new.

Honey and Mumford[8] suggested that activists should prepare themselves for training opportunities by asking themselves the following questions.

- Will I learn something new?
- Will there be a number of different activities?
- Will I be able to enjoy myself and make mistakes?
- Will I encounter some difficult challenges and problems?
- Will there be similar people to interact with?

Reflectors

Individuals who naturally reflect will prefer to:

- think or ponder over activities;
- observe group activities and meetings;
- be able to assimilate and think before acting;
- carry out research to discover;
- review activities and what they have learnt;
- produce reports and analyses;
- exchange experiences with help in a structured environment;
- avoid pressure and deadlines.

According to Honey and Mumford[9] it is important that reflectors ask themselves the following questions regarding training opportunities.

- Will there be adequate time to consider and assimilate?
- Will there be time to gather relevant information?
- Will there be the opportunity to listen to a cross-section of people's views?
- Will I be placed under pressure to produce something too quickly?

Theorists

Those who exhibit this style of learning will wish to:

- learn as part of a system, model or concept;
- have time to explore the links and relationships between ideas;

- probe the methodology, logic or idea with questions and answers;
- be intellectually challenged by being tested or through analysing a complex problem;
- have a structured session with clear guidelines;
- listen or read about ideas and concepts based on logic or a rationale;
- analyse and generalise reasons for success and failure;
- acquire interesting ideas;
- understand and participate in complex activities.

Again, Honey and Mumford[10] provide questions that learners with this style should ask themselves before attending any training or learning opportunity.

- Will there be the opportunity to ask many questions?
- Does the activity have a clear structure and purpose?
- Will I come across complex ideas and concepts designed to test me?
- Are the approaches to be explored sound and valid?
- Will there be similar individuals at the event?

Pragmatists

Individuals who lean towards this learning style will prefer to:

- see a link between the activity and their job;
- be shown techniques that have practical advantages e.g. time saving;
- have the chance to test techniques with the aid of an expert;

- be exposed to a model that they can replicate;
- be given techniques relevant to their job;
- be given opportunities to implement what they learn;
- undertake an experience based on real life or as close to as possible;
- concentrate on practical issues.

Honey and Mumford[11] suggested that pragmatists should prepare themselves for training opportunities by asking themselves the following questions.

- Will there be opportunities to practise?
- Will there be practical tips and techniques?
- Will I be looking at real scenarios that relate to my problems?
- Will there be experts available who know how to do it?

Most individuals will notice those aspects that apply to themselves and should bear these in mind when attending any form of training. Some individuals will naturally tend to be reflectors, while others will not. Learning is effective by combining different approaches, but reflection is important for the evaluation of professional development. Individuals should not ignore their own learning style, but should adapt it to improve their ability for reflection. Completing a learning-style questionnaire, such as that used by Honey and Mumford[12] will let the individual discover their own style and adapt their training and acquisition of skills accordingly.

Throughout this book reference will be made to the opportunities for training that an individual may, or may not have. Whatever opportunities the individual encounters it is important that they make the most of them.

With heavy emphasis being placed on reflection by academic institutions and by the library and information profession as an integral part of continuing professional development it is important that the individual takes appropriate steps to develop their reflective practice.

Improving reflection

There are ways in which the individual can improve their ability to reflect.

- Observe the behaviour of others, both verbal and non-verbal.
- Regularly keep a record of events and reflect on activities to see if any conclusions can be drawn from these.
- Review meetings or events and see if any lessons can be learnt from them.
- Carry out some research that requires gathering data.
- Write something that needs to be professionally presented, either a report or paper.
- Produce arguments for and against a particular course of action.

Mezey[13] points out that being reflective is not purely about evaluating training activities, it is about being effective. Employees are required to think autonomously; to create their own work; evaluate and correct their actions; and to be responsible. There are many texts that can help the library and information professional to develop their reflective practice. Mezey provides over 100 resources that have been recommended by professionals; some are from the library and information sector, but many are not.

Beyond reflection

As important as reflection is to the process of continuing professional development, the individual should not ignore or pass over opportunities for development that may present themselves. Individuals should use their own learning strengths, as emphasised in their learning style, to pursue appropriate opportunities, whether this be mentoring or attending formal academic training. Throughout this publication the individual can find ways to pursue their professional development and, more importantly, keep a record of that training for the benefit of themselves and their employer.

Sources that will aid the individual in pursuing their own personal and professional development can be located at the end of each chapter in the notes section. This includes books, serials and web sources. A true bibliography would be unwieldy for this publication and at best would not contain all the available information on professional development, much of which is not even to be found in the library and information sector. Individuals should perform some research themselves and seek out those resources that are most beneficial to them and their style of learning.

This book does not provide the answers for continuing professional development, but it does provide the individual with the guidance to control their own development and direction to enhance themselves and their careers.

Notes

1. The Quality Assurance Agency for Higher Education. *Subject Benchmarking: http://www.qaa.ac.uk/crntwork/benchmark/ benchmarking.htm* (visited 30 March 2004).

2. D. Kolb. *Continuing Professional Development: http://www1 .bcs.org.uk/bm.asp?sectionID=1047* (visited 30 March 2003).

3. Loughborough University (2000) *RAPID 2000: http://rapid .lboro.ac.uk/.* (visited 30 March 2003).

4. N. Jackson (2001) *Personal Development Planning: What Does It Mean?* PDP Working Paper 1. York: LTSN Generic Centre.

5. D.A. Schon (1982) *The Reflective Practitioner.* New York: Basic Books.

6. J. Cowan (1998) *On Becoming an Innovative University Teacher: Reflection in Action.* Buckingham: Society for Research into Higher Education and Open University Press.

7. P. Honey and A. Mumford (1986) *Using Your Learning Styles.* Maidenhead: Peter Honey.

8. Ibid., p.14

9. Ibid.

10. Ibid.

11. Ibid.

12. P. Honey and A. Mumford (1986). *The Manual of Learning Styles.* Maidenhead: Peter Honey.

13. M. Mezey (2004) A Reflective Librarian's Bookshelf. *Library and Information Update 2004*; July/August: 38–45; *http:// www.cilip.org.uk/publications/updatemagazine/archive/ archive2004/july/update0407c/* (visited 31 August 2004).

2

Skills, strengths and weaknesses

Any professional, in any field of expertise, should be aware of their own strengths and weaknesses. These can be separated into the skills the individual currently possesses and those that they wish, or need, to acquire. In the information and library profession, individuals will have varied skill-sets depending on the sector or organisation in which they operate, whether it is within the health, academic or public library and information services.

Even with comparatively diverse skill-sets, the need to consistently identify, record and develop them remains paramount. In the last 20 years the pace of technological change has been more rapid than that seen prior to the 1980s. It is therefore essential that individuals monitor their professional development and their acquisition of skills.

The Oxford English Dictionary defines skill as the 'ability to do something well'.[1] This is central to the notion of professional development in library and information science. Many skills need to be acquired but to be a professional they must be completed to an appropriate level, thus ensuring that the service delivered by an information professional is highly regarded.

To ensure that skills are acquired to the appropriate level, individuals should follow an appropriate path of continuing professional development that analyses their existing skills, including their strengths and weaknesses; builds on these and leads the individual to an increased and improved set of skills that will support their chosen career.

SWOT analysis

Strengths and weaknesses are fundamental to any individual's continuing professional development. They need to be examined and then listed both honestly and openly. Consulting with a mentor or known colleague will help to clarify this and should be as wide-ranging as possible, looking at those areas that are at present deemed to be unnecessary to current circumstances. The future may require some of these skills and where possible the professional information worker should be prepared for them. Strengths will include listings of skills and qualifications, and weaknesses will be those areas that are known to need attention to achieve any personal (or organisational) aims for the year.

Commonly strengths and weaknesses should be analysed in what is known as a SWOT analysis as described by Boydell and Leary.[2] The SWOT acronym is defined under the headings:

- strengths;
- weaknesses;
- opportunities;
- threats.

These are normally applied in an organisational setting where it is a systematic way of discovering how the organisation works and the gaps in knowledge that need to be addressed. Typical areas of investigation are staffing structures, decision-making and other processes. As part of one's own continuing professional development it is important to be aware of the organisation's needs, as this will have an obvious effect on the individual's training needs.

Performing a SWOT analysis on one's own skills is a common sense approach that will form the cornerstone of the individual's continuing professional development. The process has a slightly different context when used in a personal capacity. Strengths and weaknesses can be discovered by analysing training needs; this is detailed in the following sections. Opportunities and threats have a different perspective for the individual. Opportunities may simply be a list of possibilities or wishes that one has created, while threats may be a series of barriers that need to be overcome to attain the training or skills that have been identified.

The process of identifying strengths and weaknesses and those skills required by the individual to develop as a professional can be performed on different levels. One could simply start with a CV and note the relevant qualifications and skills found there, but to obtain a comprehensive review of these, a training-needs analysis should be performed using as much information as possible. This should not just be a voyage of discovery but also one of recording as discussed in later chapters.

Training needs analysis

The content of employee training programmes, or as they are more commonly termed in organisations today, annual development reviews or staff appraisals, is to some extent of a very similar nature. They are all designed to discover the level at which the individual is able to carry out their job functions. This is not, or should not, be in a manner that encourages those carrying out the review to use the occasion to bring pressure to bear on employees to improve performance. This is neither productive nor conducive to improving staff performance.

Using the process to analyse the training needs of individuals is the appropriate way to help both employees and organisations flourish. Training programmes can view training needs analysis in different ways. Some see the analysis as the whole process, while others see the analysis as the final part of the process when conclusions are drawn on the needs of the individual for their future development. For the purposes of this book the process is split into two distinct parts, the first being the identification of the individual's current skill-set as defined by their role within the organisation (the audit), and the second is the determination of the training necessary to meet the needs of the individual's (and the organisation's) priorities for the coming year.

Audit

Performing a training audit is the first step in the process of identifying the individual's current set of skills, the level of those skills and the resulting training needs. When determining one's own approach to self-auditing, it is important to determine one's own personal development and how it relates to the needs of the organisation by which one is employed.

Any formal process occurring in the workplace will necessarily differentiate between the individual's skills required in the workplace and personal wishes that will help to promote their career path. From a personal viewpoint it will be necessary to make this distinction, so that one's career is taken forward independently of the employing organisation. This said, improving one's skills in the workplace will improve the service to be offered to the user, whatever your speciality, whether systems, cataloguing or front-of-house delivery. The process of auditing should, therefore, consider both aspects separately, i.e. the needs of the organisation and the individual.

There are many ways that information to support this process can be sourced. Those suggested below are drawn from an original list provided by Williamson[3] and then amended to cater for the current working environment. They can provide a substantial amount of data for both the individual and the organisation which can be used to identify skills acquired and future training needs. The list is not exclusive and anyone creating a portfolio or record to support their professional development should always keep this in mind:

- training budgets
- organisational structures
- aims and objectives
- strategic plans
- job descriptions
- training/appraisal records
- course outlines
- user surveys
- questionnaires
- interviews
- observation.

Each of these can provide considerable help when identifying those skills that have already been identified and those that will be required in the foreseeable future to meet the needs of the organisation and the individual.

Training budgets

This can play a crucial role in the whole training process. Some library and information units do not have any budget for staff training while others will have no facilities for course fees, but will pay travel and subsistence. This will differ from country to country and even more so at a more local level. The availability of funds to support individuals in their development can limit the outcomes of the process. Whatever the level of funding it is certain that not all training needs of all employees can be satisfied in any one year. This means that priorities will have to be decided before allocating funds to training. If these are limited then the individual must pursue their own development vigorously through their own means. This will be addressed in later chapters.

Organisational structures

In any organisation, the activities of one part of the institution can impact on another. In a large library service, different sections will affect one another, for example, the systems librarian(s) will need to align their activities with the librarians who deliver resources. In a smaller environment with a single-staffed library (solo librarian or other similar description), the impact of the organisation is more immediate, with other departments, such as marketing, making direct requests of the individual librarian. The different facets of an organisation's business will result in different internal dynamics within the organisation that will have an impact on the training needs of library staff.

Aims and objectives

The organisation will have its own aims and objectives to which the library or information service will also adhere. In many cases they will also have a further set of aims and objectives that will be distinct from the parent organisation but will support their mission. It is unlikely that any organisation operating in the current environment does not have their own aims and objectives, but where they do not, or where the individual's department does not, then it is important to gather any related documentation that confirms the needs of the organisation.

Strategic plans

This documentation is equally important to the individual as aims and objectives. The strategic plan of any organisation provides a clear indication of its future direction and consequently will also provide an insight into the skills of the workforce that will need to be enhanced or developed. If, for example, the institution is planning to roll out a new IT system where there was previously none then there will be the need to ensure that all employees develop the requisite IT skills to perform their role. These documents, together with aims and objectives, will help provide guidance on the organisation's needs and hence the individual's training needs.

Job descriptions

Most jobs now have job descriptions attached to them as a matter of course. This part of the recruitment process enables applicants to determine whether their skill-set fulfils the requirements of the post. Typically, the job description provides a clear picture of the intended purpose, tasks and responsibilities of the post. It is possible that a job description does not exist, for example where a post has been in existence for many years and did not originally have a description; in such instances one should be created, as they are imperative to enable the evaluation of the job and the development of staff. Further to the creation of descriptions it is also important that these are reviewed and updated to maintain their currency.

Similarly, person specifications are an important tool that will help to provide evidence towards training needs. They describe the personal qualities, experience and qualifications expected of the individual who is qualified to fill the post.

These two sets of documents will go a long way towards helping to define the skills necessary for a particular role and will clarify gaps in the organisation's strategic documents relating to hierarchies and responsibilities. Although they will help to define the skill-set, other documents are necessary to help to determine the issue as to the level of skills the individual has already obtained.

Training/appraisal records

As mentioned previously in this chapter, staff appraisal and other methods of recording staff development are an essential tool for determining training needs. Part of the formal process within organisations to monitor the effectiveness of staff training records and staff appraisals provides a record of training undertaken by individuals. These are sometimes distinctly separate documents within an organisation, but they are also often merged as part of the same evaluative process. More apparent and consistent record keeping in institutions is resulting in record keeping that supports the identification of training needs for both the individual and the organisation. Training records may or may not be stored with individual's personnel records and will provide a listing of all training that has been attended or pursued previously. They might also contain details on whether this has been successful or otherwise and will depend on the particular circumstances of the individual. This information may or may not be readily available to those involved in library training, but it is available to the individual. Everyone is entitled to access to their own records and should keep copies for themselves so as to plan their own personal development. This is of more importance in the current climate as it will provide the key for the individual to be able to develop continually as a professional.

Staff appraisal records, or their equivalent such as performance measurement, record the individual's progress in their capacity as an employee. Again, these records will only work effectively if they are available. Modern organisational schemes can achieve this by storing the entire appraisal record with the individual's personnel file, but provide a separate sheet of recorded training needs which is available to those responsible for library budgets and training, including line managers. This will often differ depending on the sector, but those in UK higher education echo this model. Although this sheet will not contain great detail it provides scope (and room) for the expression of individual needs.

Course outlines

Although not generally recognised in training texts, outlines of courses and training events that have been attended and even detailed papers are exceptionally useful in completing records at a later stage. The detail they provide can be used to complete personal development records in whatever form and, on a more opportunistic level, can be used to inform CVs and job application forms. They can also provide information for any collation of training needs in organisational reviews, such as staff appraisals, although this will be minimal compared with the information that can be added by the individual to their own personal recording systems. Skills obtained as a result of the course are likely to be expressed in the course's learning outcomes and if the course is assessed in any way, then the results will provide an indication of the individual's level of competency in those skills.

User surveys

Some training manuals that discuss the identification of training needs espouse the use of customer complaints as a way of identifying the training needs of individuals within the organisation. This is a very negative way of dealing with employees and should be discouraged as it is often difficult to differentiate between a genuine complaint and a disgruntled user who possibly did not get the item they requested. There is, however, merit in using user surveys to determine areas in which the library or information service should improve or provide a new service that is needed by users. For example, installing a new phone renewal system in an institution's library service will necessitate both technical staff and frontline counter staff to learn new skills to deal with users' issues upon delivery. They can be particularly useful in determining patterns of use, misuse or service improvements which would benefit the organisation. Users can often provide an objective view of the organisation's service provision.

Questionnaires

Specific circumstances within an organisation may precipitate the use of questionnaires to help determine the level of skills within the library service. This would be specific to the library service and independent of the formal appraisal process but could be exceptionally useful in improving the service given to users within the organisation. Using questionnaires to ascertain the perceived training needs of staff can provide information on educational achievements, goals and gaps within skills and training. Ostensibly though, questionnaires will be used to discover if there are any patterns in training needs within library and information services. For example, a questionnaire completed by a number of staff may indicate that they are uncomfortable dealing with users' queries on a virtual learning environment (VLE). This would obviously indicate a need to inform and educate staff on what it is and how it works, to make them more effective as frontline staff.

There are many ways and means for collecting information through questionnaires, which will be dependent on what information is intended to be collected and collated. There are a number of standard forms and tests, such as the Belbin team roles questionnaire which could be used in certain circumstances. However, there is likely to be greater merit in producing a questionnaire locally, to provide the exact information required for the organisation, and also, even if only as a side effect, further information for the individual's personal development. Useful examples can be found in many sectors including those used by public authorities and illustrated by Williamson.[4] Publications already exist on writing questionnaires for library and information research and when creating one for yourself or your institution it is worth referring to Busha and Harter[5] and Bell.[6]

Interviews

This is really an additional method of data collection and is used in a similar way to both appraisals and questionnaires. Information on training needs may be elicited in a more open and conducive manner by using interviews. Staff appraisals may include both an interview and questionnaire, as the questionnaire will provide factual information, while the interview will provide information on the individual's perceptions. The interview can produce more useful data as the interviewer is able to put the individual at their ease and may elicit information that would not have been placed on a form. It is entirely probable that the interviewee may not have realised that they had a need for a particular skill or even that they were in possession of certain skills.

Observation

Directly observing someone can provide information on whether an individual has training needs. Observing routine tasks can both show deficiencies of the individual and whether they excel in a particular role. Much can depend on the observer, someone familiar to the observee would possibly make the process less daunting. It is, however, difficult to use this for less frequent activities as they are unlikely to occur during the observation period. Self-observation is possible if a log is completed by the individual on how they are performing tasks. From this it may be possible to identify areas of training need.

All of these methods offer the individual opportunities to gather data to develop a collective description of their own set of skills, built up and maintained over an increasing period of time. It is unlikely that any one person will have collated information using all of these methods but will combine a selection from their place of work or from records in their own possession. These records may reach back over a period of years and would include details from documents relating to a first degree and any subsequent professional qualifications, not forgetting any relevant work experience both following and preceding these.

The individual and the employer must together use these records to ensure that any recording of training and skills is both current and up-to-date. Most employers today will operate schemes that record training undertaken and skills both upgraded and added during their tenure in the post. This information together with that personally kept by the individual should be organised in an appropriate manner to ensure that a full description of their skills is recorded to enable them to continually develop as a professional. One such way is to create a portfolio that the individual can continuously update. The following chapters will furnish further information and guidance on this topic. Comparing one's own collection of skills, as collated, with existing schemes may also help identify missing skills in one's own area of work. For example TFPL Ltd., a consultancy firm, based in the UK, have published the *Knowledge Management Competency Dictionary*,[7] which provides descriptions of the key skills and competencies that are required for success in this branch of information work. The US Special Libraries Association[8] has published a document detailing competencies for special librarians, another example of an extremely useful source against which one's own skills can be measured. Individuals can use this as a guide to skills that they wish to develop. Others do already exist and many professional bodies around the world provide frameworks for skills development. The emphasis here is on continuity: to achieve any kind of consistency and to identify which skills and what training to undertake, the process must be periodically reviewed on an annual or more frequent basis.

Analysis

Identifying the appropriate documentation is the first step in enabling the individual to determine the skills they have. Collating the records into a single portfolio will make future identification a simpler process. Following the identification of skills, the next stage of the development process is to analyse the resulting skills and the gaps that exist within them. These will be personal objectives for the coming year or more if it is a longer-term plan.

The following questions regarding training needs, drawn and amended from work by Williamson,[9] are now ready to be addressed.

- What training is needed?
- Why is it necessary?
- In what form will it be delivered?
- Where and who will provide it?

What training is needed?

Having analysed the documentation pertinent to the individual's skills and performance, they will have (or should have) a list of skills they need to acquire or improve and, hence, a set of training needs. Not all of these (depending on how many) can be carried out in a single year, but a set of objectives for the year should be created so that a plan is set for that period. This gives momentum to the plan and the individual. It is likely that these needs will actually be a mixture of education and training.

Why is it necessary?

Prioritising one's needs is paramount. From time-management to word-processing skills, it is important to know why the skill is being acquired and what need it will satisfy; will it satisfy a need that the employer has within the library or information service or is it a personal objective aimed at building a new path for one's career. Whatever the reason, ensure that it meets a real need. It is all too easy to attend a training session because one can and not because it is a genuine need. Some organisations provide internal training that brings staff together but may not be directly relevant to their role. This can lead to frustration if the individual does not get to use this training. Conversely, individuals can be made to feel left out if training is delivered to some staff but not others. Taking advantage of opportunities is fine, but only if appropriate. This should be considered carefully by line managers as a matter of course, but individuals should be aware of this and bear in mind their real needs. Training is wasted if it is not to be used in the course of the individual's professional activities.

How will it be delivered?

There are many ways that training can be delivered and, more importantly, individuals will learn in different ways. Pinpointing the most appropriate method of learning for each individual is necessary if the training is going to be effective.

The list of possible training methods will include:

- case studies;
- computer-assisted learning aids (such as CD-based tutorials);
- demonstrations;
- discussions;
- e-learning (such as that provided through VLEs);
- external courses;
- focus groups;
- internal courses;
- job shadowing;
- lectures;
- observations;
- on-the-job training;
- open (or flexible) learning;
- professional reading;
- role play;
- secondments;
- visits;
- workshops.

All of these methods can be used by the individual when undergoing training to acquire new skills. The effectiveness of the learning undertaken will depend on the preferred learning style of the individual and its availability to them. Training that involves practical aspects of the work is characterised by 'behavioural style learning'. Those who learn best through this method might improve their skills by attending practical workshops or other 'hands-on' experiences. Alternatively those who prefer to learn in a 'cognitive style' will prefer attending more traditional lectures or learning through role-playing. Sometimes the content of the programme will determine the style, for example, essions on decision making will require a more cognitive style. Often a combination of the both behavioural and cognitive styles will be employed in professional training scenarios.

Where and who will provide it?

The question of where and who will provide training is no small task. Many factors can affect the delivery of training for the individual. They may be able to benefit from any of the above methods, such as university courses or internal courses run by the employing organisation, but other factors will have a bearing on any training that is undertaken. On occasion, training will need to take place in the workplace or alternatively would be better placed in a different environment to facilitate learning.

Support from the employing organisation is always important and can make the difference between undertaking training or foregoing it. For example, some Microsoft training courses undertaken by systems librarians can be prohibitively expensive for the individual, as can some university courses, such as the Master of Business Administration (MBA), for librarians moving into management. It may therefore be more appropriate, where possible, to attend internal courses within the organisation. If the organisation's training budget cannot meet immediate needs for external courses then it may make available training using its own staff, if cost effective. This raises another point regarding the cost of courses to the organisation. If a course is expensive then the organisation must evaluate whether the cost of the course is worth paying in relation to the benefit they will receive and the needs that it will meet. This is also worth bearing in mind by the individual; investing a disproportionate amount of time and money in training for what may be little return could be a waste of their time and resources. Another way of acquiring these skills should, therefore, be sought. Other alternatives for those training on a limited budget may also be appropriate to different individual circumstances and will be addressed in later chapters.

The time taken for a course of study or session may also be a deciding factor when arranging training for one or for joint training sessions with colleagues. Time can be crucial: there are a number of elements that might affect the progress of the individual's professional development. Everyone within an organisation will need training and can expect to be allowed to attend courses relevant to them. This can cause difficulties for the organisation because if one person is on a training course and not at their post, then their post will need to be covered during their absence. For this reason it is unlikely that a number of individuals from one organisation would attend the same course. There are exceptions to this of course, because if the training is sufficiently generic, for example, a course on leadership, then individuals from different departments may be able to attend together. This is more likely in large organisations such as those found in local government. From an individual's perspective, the time required to undertake training can also be prohibitive. Attending a single day's training at an event organised by the professional body, of which there are many across the globe, is very different from attending one day a week or an evening to complete an educational course, such as a further degree. The circumstances of the individual will dictate how much and how often they can put into their professional development.

The types of materials used in the learning process may also determine the training undertaken by the individual, though in some cases the circumstances in which the individual finds themselves at any particular time during their career may determine the choice of training and materials. As previously mentioned, time is very precious for those already employed, or with family commitments, thus time dedicated to training must be carefully chosen. In these circumstances the most appropriate methods may involve open or distance learning where the materials are provided by an institution and the learner can pace themselves. There are also times when training materials in the form of course packs, manuals or CDs to name a few are preferable to courses at fixed times and places. Some training materials can be expensive but it is possible that others in your organisation may already have some of the required materials available for you to borrow. Current methods of learning are changing; higher education and some business arenas are introducing e-learning. This will become more widespread and will enable learners to pace their own learning to some extent. E-learning can take different forms. It may take the form of a VLE, such as Blackboard or WebCT; an institutional intranet; or a computer-based training aid, such as a CD or software program.

Individuals will also be affected by their (or their organisation's) present or future need. Situations in which this might arise include new legal requirements, such as copyright law and disability legislation. These might present an immediate need for re-skilling for both the individual and the organisation. Whether for this reason or another, many situations will arise, such as the introduction of new technology, needing either an instant reaction or some proactivity on the part of the individual. In cases where the need is imminent then the individual (and the employer) will need to ensure that the service provided does not suffer by providing some form of skills updating on short notice. Where more time is available there is an opportunity to be proactive, but this still needs to be tempered with some caution; if training is provided too far in advance then it may be forgotten long before it is needed in practice. Careful planning can lead to the improvement of skills for the individual and delivery of a professional service for the employer.

Organisational objectives, if similar to those of the individual, can be attached to the professional development programme of the individual and included in their annual objectives. This is highly beneficial as it can result in a programme of continuing professional development for the year which is supported by the organisation and the individual with the possible further benefits of support in terms of both time and money.

Summary

Ensuring that they have the right skills for the post they are in and for the career path they have mapped out for themselves is the responsibility of every professional. Continuing professional development means being able to look at one's own strengths and weaknesses across the skills they possess and those they wish to develop. This requires planning to a considerable degree to enable the individual to keep up-to-date with changes in their working environment and to put in place the building blocks that will further their career. Rapid and continuous changes in technology pose particular problems for the development of skills for the individual. Software packages are released with new features on a frequent basis and the speed with which information is processed grows every year with the development of new processors in computers. It is therefore doubly important to keep up-to-date and to develop one's skills.

This is a process that requires planning over time. This chapter has shown how to think about the skills individuals have and how to begin to plan for their development in the future. The first step is the SWOT analysis which requires looking at the different areas of an individual's skills development, these being strengths, weaknesses, opportunities and threats. Normally used in an organisational context this simple acronym is a useful starting point to begin thinking about what each person does best and what they need to improve, to perform at an accepted level as an information professional. It also makes us think about the methods employed by ourselves to achieve some of the training needs once any deficits have been found in the individual's skills levels.

A detailed training needs audit and analysis, as described above, is a time-consuming process but should be carried out by the dedicated information professional. This should not be performed in a short period of time or on just a single occasion. It is a process that should be carefully and deliberately carried out so that the individual knows which skills they have attained to a high level and which skills they need to develop to improve their effectiveness at work and to improve their job prospects in the future. The training needs analysis provides a method for doing this by using existing information to be found both at home and in the workplace.

The frequency of the training needs analysis should be performed on an annual basis, with a more frequent 'check' carried out on a six-monthly basis to determine whether the training programme that has been devised is on schedule to be completed and that the original training needs are still appropriate. It is likely that in the right circumstances the introduction of new technology, or new staff with different skill-sets, can change the needs of the organisation and the individuals.

Using these methods and sources of information the skills, strengths and weaknesses of the individual can be ascertained. Once discovered and, equally importantly, recorded, then it is possible to plan the development of the individual's skills and the training programme needed to be adopted to achieve this.

Notes

1. *The Oxford Paperback Dictionary.* 3rd edn (1988) Oxford: Oxford University Press.
2. T. Boydell and M. Leary (1986) *Identifying Training Needs.* London: Institute of Personnel and Development.
3. M. Williamson (1993) *Training Needs Analysis.* London: Library Association Publishing.
4. Ibid.
5. C.H. Busha and S.P. Harter (1980) *Research Methods in Librarianship: Techniques and Interpretation.* New York; London: Academic Press.
6. J. Bell (1999) *Doing Your Research Project: A Guide for First-Time Researchers in Education and Social Science.* 3rd edn Buckingham: Open University Press.
7. *Knowledge and Information Management Competency Dictionary* (2003) London: TFPL.
8. J. Marshall, B. Fisher, L. Moulton and R. Piccoli. (1996) *Competencies for Special Librarians of the 21st Century.* Washington: Special Libraries Association.
9. M. Williamson, *op cit.*

3

Using portfolios to record professional development

Why build a portfolio? Is it to gain accreditation to a professional organisation or is to develop one's own skills? This may seem like a straightforward question, but it is more complex than this. Building one's own set of skills is inextricably linked to accreditation of a professional body. An important aspect of building a portfolio is to gather evidence that gives an indication of our own personal level of skills. This may lead to the position of the individual being able to submit themselves for professional accreditation, but this should be a by-product of the process – the most important thing to remember is that it is about developing one's professional skills. However, every individual has to begin from a single point to address the development of new skills or the improvement of older ones. To do this it is necessary to assess oneself against a clearly defined set of criteria. Criteria laid down by professional associations and other organisations can be used by the individual to help to build their own portfolios. Examples of skills criteria will be examined in this chapter.

Identifying one's training needs is a long and laborious task and it requires sifting through a considerable body of documentation, both physical (printed) and virtual (electronic). To ensure that nothing is lost during this process it is vital that it is recorded in some way. There is, therefore, a need for a clear statement of the skill-set, and for benchmarks against which a professional practitioner can judge both their level of competency and their need for further training and skill acquisition. Projects over the last ten years have focused upon, and examined the skills of information professionals. For example, the Skills for new Information Professionals (SKIP) project,[1] based at the University of Plymouth, looked at the technological skills gaps of library and information staff and attempted to define the nature and type of IT skills for information professionals. However, projects of this type have never produced a comprehensive set of skills that relate to those needed by the information professional of the twenty-first century.

The UK Information Services National Training Organisation (ISNTO) has developed detailed standards for National Vocational Qualifications (NVQs) up to and including degree level.[2] These can be used by those under-taking NVQs at work in information and library services. These standards cover the practical facets of information work, but do not give enough detail on the theoretical aspects, which are very much a part of education in departments of information and library science, and that are also seen as important by employers.

A need, therefore, exists for a method of recording that supports all of these aspects of the rounded information professional's career. Any recording system used to track the individual's skills development must incorporate both the theoretical and practical aspects of the professional skill-set. As professionals it is incumbent upon us to take individual control of our own professional development and record that development. The best way is by carrying out an audit of our skills, as described in the previous chapter, and then by recording it in the form of a portfolio.

Portfolios can be created in any manner the individual wishes, since they fulfil the needs of the individual's professional development and not the needs of the employing organisation or even the professional association. A portfolio will necessarily include both the employer's and professional association's requirements plus any additional developmental needs that the individual believes will benefit them either in their present or future careers. The increasing widening of the information profession, as described by John Feather[3] in the Charted Institute of Library and Information Professionals (CILIP) journal, is leading to an increasingly disparate set of skills for information professionals depending on the sector within which they are working. It is unlikely that any recording system developed through any project or professional organisation will fulfil the needs of most information professionals. This does not negate the use of recording systems or portfolios that have been developed. These will be especially useful as the basis of a recording system for skills development, but as professionals we must expand on them to record the skills, or higher levels of skills, that they do not cover. Building a portfolio that includes these essentials is not an easy or small task, but neither should it be, as it will be a mechanism for ensuring continuous professional development.

What makes a portfolio?

The impetus for the creation of a portfolio and for the recording of skills must come from the individual. This requires that they take full control of the process themselves.

Organisation

To be successful at creating a portfolio one has to be exceptionally well organised. This requires keeping a copy of all relevant documents as they are produced and continuously collecting and collating material. Most of these have been described in the previous chapter and, most importantly, should be collected from the earliest moment possible. This could be from the moment one first begins employment or, as is more likely, from the moment when our professional education begins at university or college. It is difficult at first to know what to collect and initially it is probably wise to collect everything. This could be daunting and it will leave the individual wondering how to organise all the collected material. Simple organisational methods such as date order, may be appropriate in the first instance, and can be used until such time as an appropriate structure can be found from either an external source or from the identification of skills through a personal audit. Once sufficient organisation has been given to the documents that have been collated then any gaps in the individual's skills and hence documentation will be clear.

Time

Never underestimate the considerable amount of time required to organise a portfolio. Employers can be very considerate and some will allow their employees time during work to compete their portfolio. Even with this consideration it will still require the individual to put in a large amount of their own time. If the portfolio is being used to gain professional status, as is the case in the UK, then it may require using holiday entitlement to complete everything by a designated deadline.

Sorting of the evidence that has been collected is one of the most time-consuming activities. Copious amounts of paper (and other formats) must be brought together and then be made accessible for future use by arranging it in a series of files or other methods of storage. This deals with the physical aspects of the evidence, but further to this, it is important that any evidence, descriptive notes or annotations used in the portfolio are proof-read and edited. Other work on the presentation and layout of the portfolio will also take time, especially the process of creating and sorting page numbering and a system for recording the pieces of evidence to be included. This can be extremely problematic especially where different formats are involved, such as audio-visual materials and computer-based formats. It is possible to make suggestions on how to do this, whether to use page numbers or record numbers or both, but there is no right way to do this. The most important thing to ensure is that the evidence can be easily located from the portfolio's contents section.

Planning

Planning may be the most important aspect of creating a portfolio. If insufficient time is given over to planning the structure then it is highly likely that considerable changes will have to be made to restructure the portfolio at a later date. Data should be assiduously collected before deciding the shape the structure should take in its final form. There are many decisions to be made regarding the portfolio, including the length of time it is to cover, the type of material to include, how it will be indexed and what accompanying notes must be generated. For example, when deciding on the period of time covered, this will be dictated by the individual's needs. A new professional may well create a portfolio to achieve some form of accreditation with a professional body. Others, however, will have been professionally active in the workplace for a considerably longer period of time. They will be more interested in lifelong learning; developing their skills and with it their careers. Much of this will be dictated by the style and method of working favoured by the individual – creating a portfolio is a hard task, which need not be further complicated by working in a different way.

Structure

Although there is not a wealth of material on building portfolios in library and information science, it is beneficial to take a look at other portfolios and to locate books and articles about portfolios to help with the structure. Once researched this information should enable the identification of a suitable structure to be adopted. Deciding on the appropriate structure and adopting a method to make it work is a skill in itself and will aid the professional development process. Remember that the material may fit one structure better than another and it supports the individual's own professional development, so it is more important that the structure supports the evidence of the individual's own skills development. What should be ensured, however, is that the portfolio is clear, concise, easily accessible and meets the relevant criteria for skills development.

Professionals should not hesitate to discuss their portfolio with line managers, mentors or even peers. Many will have built their own portfolios or followed another method of professional development and will therefore be a great source of ideas and information regarding professional development. They may even be involved in the assessment process at some point, which can make their input even more valuable to the individual. This should provide some insight into possible problems that may arise with a chosen structure or even pinpoint some areas that have been so far omitted. More importantly it may provide some solutions to questions raised by the individual regarding their portfolio creation.

Tools

It may be that the structure is predetermined by the organisation with which you are associated, or if not, they may provide a tool that can be used to help in this process. In the UK, for example, the Chartered Institute of Library and Information Professionals provides a framework for continuing professional development.[4] As a tool this is not supposed to provide the complete solution to all professional development needs but it can help to guide the individual in examining their own needs and aid them in finding the structure that best suits them and their way of working. There are other sources of tools and these should also be utilised, from whichever country they arose, the skills content still remains valid.

Selectivity

Once the portfolio is underway then it is important to analyse the material that has been collected. Not all of it can be used in the portfolio as this would be unsustainable for many reasons, not least of which would be its size. It is important that the individual is particularly selective regarding the material they include. Only material relevant to the skills or criteria being addressed should be included, whatever format it may take.

When building a portfolio it is most important to remember that it is quality, not quantity, which will make the portfolio a successful tool for continuing professional development. To ensure that the material selected achieves the appropriate levels of quality required for professional development and for accreditation, five simple checks, as shown below, can be used when sifting through evidence.

Evidence

All evidence gathered by the individual to support their professional development should, according to many writers on portfolio development (see Simosko[5] and Redman[6]) include evidence that is:

- valid;
- reliable;
- sufficient;
- authentic;
- current.

Validity is key to the evidence collected by the individual. The individual must ask themselves if the material they have collected addresses the criteria as laid down in the skills statement or accreditation document. Further to this, does the selected material actually demonstrate the individual's competency, or does it add nothing to that which has previously been collected? The aim of building a portfolio is to address the individual's training needs and develop their skills, thus it is vital that the evidence helps meet these needs.

When the portfolio is assessed, those responsible for examining the evidence need to be reassured that it is reliable. This means that the material collected by the individual conveys the same meaning to the assessor as to themselves.

This is not an easy task, especially if the eventual assessors are unknown and/or remote; however, by talking to peers, mentors and line managers, the individual can get a sense of whether the evidence does reliably meet the required criteria.

Is there sufficient information in the portfolio to provide a picture of the individual's level of competency? A balance needs to be struck between how much material is too much, or too little, to give a clear indication that one has indeed met the required standards. If a piece of evidence appears to repeat something that has already been added to the portfolio then it is unnecessary, simply referring to the other piece is all that is required.

The portfolio is meant to show the competencies of the individual concerned and as such it is important that the evidence contained within is authentic and the work of the individual concerned. Material produced as part of a group is appropriate, but the role played by the individual must be clear within the evidence so that anyone who may assess the portfolio is completely clear on the skills that have been demonstrated.

Lastly, it is important that the evidence presented represents the current level of individual's skills. If the material in the portfolio is a few years old then it must be clearly demonstrated that the appropriate level of skills has been maintained by the individual in the current period of time. If this does not appear to be the case then evidence of a more recent nature should be collected and inserted into the portfolio.

It could be argued that specificity should be added to the five checks suggested by other writers. The evidence that is collected must be specific to the skills or competencies that the individual is in the process of proving they have acquired. It is not remotely adequate to use evidence that relates to another skill and also vaguely relates to the skill being addressed. This should also be borne in mind when selecting evidence.

These five checks are crucial to the successful selection of evidence for inclusion in the portfolio. If these are adhered to then the individual should be able to show that they have met the criteria required by any body for accreditation. This is not an easy task, as it requires careful consideration to ensure that the correct evidence is selected. Do not be afraid to approach colleagues or line managers for their opinion as this will undoubtedly help to refine one's own sense of the appropriateness of material.

What to include?

When beginning to create a portfolio the emphasis should be on collecting material from the outset. It is important to hold on to as much material as possible at this stage, and then later sift the material, introducing the five criteria noted above. As a guide the following types of information should be included as essential in a portfolio, as they will help to frame the individual's personal situation and continuing professional development needs.

- CV including job titles and descriptions;
- evidence on recent skills development;
- annotated contents;
- an objective, evaluative introduction;
- aims and objectives of the employing organisation (and understanding);
- examples of commitment to continuing professional development (CPD);

- understanding of, and involvement with the professional body;
- details of relevant learning/training;
- identification of strengths and weaknesses;
- bibliography;
- listing of visits and courses.

This list is not exclusive; the materials suggested in Chapter 2 are evidence that there is scope to add more, or rather different, subject matter when creating the portfolio. As a general rule these headings are a useful starting point for anyone embarking on a record of their own professional development.

Evidence

How are these broad headings to be populated? Evidence from a wide ranging series of sources should be employed. Those below are again a selection of possible materials that individuals may wish to include as evidence of personal and professional development:

- examples of work;
- journal;
- responses to enquiries from users/colleagues;
- project involvement;
- publicity created;
- photographs;
- reports (meetings, evaluations);
- letters/memoranda;
- guidance notes to staff/users;

- contributions to professional press;
- training (evaluation forms);
- personal reports (meetings, events, visits);
- case studies;
- testimonies/observations;
- multimedia.

Examples of work

This may seem like a strange heading, as nearly everything could come under this, indeed many of the suggestions that follow could be seen as 'examples of work'. However, it should be noted that this refers particularly to the workplace and as such some of the following may not be restricted solely to the workplace. For example, duty rosters which indicate a level of planning and organisation can be included, as could planning notes for a project or an event.

Journal

It is valid and extremely useful to keep a regular journal of one's activities. Writing up frequent journal entries that correspond to experiences will enable the individual to return at a later date and reflect on what they have done. Notes made at the time of the activity will remind the individual exactly how they felt at the time.

Responses to enquiries from users/colleagues

Queries received from users of an information service may take place on a verbal, written or even electronic level. Keeping a record of these responses can be used to show how an enquiry was handled and the skills that were employed during the process. Any correspondence used during the process of answering problems for users and colleagues will provide good evidence of the level of skill that the user has employed in their work.

Project involvement

Project work is a good way of demonstrating the development of new skills. This can range from a small project based in a local environment, such as the provision of a selection of book titles based on a particular topic and then promoting them to users, to a large project that may be a national project or consortium researching particular information needs within diverse ethnic groups. Much of the work done in a project setting may well be carried out by a group rather than an individual. In these circumstances it is important to make clear within the portfolio exactly what the individual's role has been by including explanatory annotations with the evidence.

Publicity

Promotional materials that have been created as part of an event or to inform users about an underused or new service are especially useful as evidence within a portfolio. This is for two reasons; first, they provide an indication of the individual's skill at producing publicity materials whether it is through the use of desktop publishing materials or through other methods, such as display boards. Second, at the same time they also indicate that the individual has been involved in the work of a project. The project concerned may be holding an event or carrying out some research, all of which need to be publicised at some point. Again the use of explanatory notes with the evidence helps to give a fuller picture of the individual's contribution.

Photographs

Professionals may not initially feel that photographs have a place in a portfolio, but there is no reason why not. Publicity, reviewed above, gives the opportunity to show how useful photographs can be when used as evidence when recording professional development. If a display board has been created it is difficult to provide evidence of what has been created unless a photograph (or digital image) is taken. They can also be useful if the library or information environment has been changed to provide ergonomically better accommodation for users or staff. Sparing a few moments thought to the possible uses of images in a portfolio could help to provide more attractive and more informative evidence.

Reports

Meeting and evaluation reports will contain vital evidence of skills that the professional can refer to in a portfolio. If the report mentions the individual by name and the role they have played in any aspect of work then it points to a level they have attained. Alternatively, if the individual has written the report themselves then it provides evidence of their competency in report writing and evaluation, as well as their role in the work.

Letters/memoranda

Correspondence in the form of letters or memoranda from colleagues, line managers, and external contacts will help to indicate the work that has been done by the individual. Their role will be clear from the correspondence and the success of their personal input can be gleaned from this form of evidence.

Guidance notes

Staff and users are the recipients of instructions or guidance notes that have been prepared by someone who is responsible for a particular aspect of the information service. These notes are further evidence of the individual's mastery of this area of information provision, making them exceptionally pertinent to the portfolio.

Professional press

Any contributions that the individual has made to the professional press need to be included in a portfolio. They are useful for many reasons, for example they could indicate that the writer has acquired knowledge in a particular area, or that they are reporting on an event that they have attended. Whatever the content of the writing concerned it will be useful if only to show that the individual can write and express themselves cogently. Those new to the library and information profession, reading this and thinking they are unlikely to produce anything for the press at this stage of their careers should think again. Many professional groups have their own publications or newsletters and are always looking for material to fill their pages. Do not feel abashed at approaching editors and offering to write a book review, or write up an event or training course one has attended. Whatever it is, remember that not everything published has to be a two thousand words (or more) article on a specialist area. Start on a smaller scale and then work up, it is all part of continuing professional development.

Training (evaluation forms)

Any course or training that is attended should have some kind of outcome. Hopefully the outcome is that the individual has improved their skills level or acquired a new skill. However, this is not necessarily so, the outcome may be less desirable and the training a waste of time. Despite this, some lessons should be learnt from the event. As a matter of course the individual should complete an evaluation form for each event they attend to record their thoughts at the time. They can then reflect on how they have benefited from it when they come to include it in their portfolio. This will provide a more solid base from which they can decide how they will move forward with their skills development.

Personal reports

As part of one's professional development and changing roles within the workplace it is likely that the individual will attend meetings, events and visits. Many of these will require that they are reported back to the line manager, or the team in which one works, either in written or verbal form. It is good practice to write them up, as they act as evidence that can be referred to in a portfolio and in some cases also allow the individual to reflect, as with the training evaluation forms, on what was achieved at the meeting or visit.

Case studies

To capture the essence of a project or an event at work (not training) then the use of a case study could provide good evidence for a portfolio. Writing up the sequence of events from the planning stage, through the implementation, to a review of the finished product will allow the professional to reflect on the processes involved and draw their own conclusions on which aspects could have been improved and those areas that were particularly successful. Included as part of a portfolio, it will be possible to make annotated links to the case study for many skills and competencies.

Testimonies/observations

One of the best forms of evidence is the testimony of a fellow professional. This could be a line manager, mentor or a peer. If a colleague has worked with you on a project or has seen you carrying out a particular activity, such as an enquiry desk session, then it would be entirely appropriate to ask them to write up what they have seen. The benefit of this type of evidence is that it is not the individual's opinion of their competency, but that of another professional which has considerable weight as it is an independent assessment.

Multimedia

Many do not think of including multimedia materials in their portfolios – certainly, it would be cumbersome to include a video cassette or a floppy disk in what is largely a paper file. Despite this it can add immensely to the understanding of anyone who reviews the portfolio, as they can see the whole of the presentation or event as it happens. It can, however, have its drawbacks. First, it is difficult to make links from a paper-based portfolio to 'somewhere' on a disk or videotape and second, restrictions may be placed on individuals by legislation, for example the UK Data Protection Act 1984[7] restricts the reporting of public events unless permission is gained from all parties.

Annotating the evidence

It should not be assumed that any piece of evidence included in a portfolio can be understood without explanatory notes attached to it. If the evidence is to be meaningful to those viewing the portfolio then annotations must be made to each piece. Each annotation should convey the following information:

- exactly what the evidence is;
- who created it;
- when it was created;
- why it was created;
- what the evidence shows;
- keywords.

The first four should be on every piece of evidence, but the last two will depend upon the purpose of the portfolio, but should be used anyway as it is good practice. If the portfolio is being used to demonstrate professional development to an employer or professional body then explaining what development the evidence shows is crucial, and keywords are useful if the portfolio is to be successfully interrogated. Keywords enable the individual to index the portfolio more effectively.

Structuring the portfolio

A portfolio can be structured in a number of ways to show the development of the individual. This applies to both personal and professional development and at any stage in one's career, whether as a student or as a member of senior management. There are a few possibilities regarding structure, the following four are suggested by Baume:[8]

- time;
- individual pieces of work;
- topic or theme;
- learning outcome or assessment criteria.

Although not all may be the most appropriate for continuing professional development. The individual will make the ultimate decision themselves and should choose the approach that best fits their way of working.

Time

Organising by chronological order is one of the easiest ways of structuring a portfolio, largely because the evidence is placed sequentially in the portfolio as it is acquired. This is a good way of showing how some skills have developed over time. However, a very good system of annotations must be put in place to accompany this. For example, if one needs to demonstrate how one has developed in a particular area then one must be able to go straight to the correct evidence, which can only be achieved if a good indexing system has been used.

Individual pieces of work

It could be appropriate to demonstrate a series of projects or events and collate the work for each together, such as planning notes or correspondence, to show how skills were used and/or developed during that time. This can be useful, but perhaps not entirely apt for professional development, as other criteria may be useful as seen below.

Topic or theme

This is likely to provide a better basis on which to build a portfolio for professional development. Topics or themes can be based on areas or aspects of the work that the individual does, for example, information literacy, enquiry work and web page development. For the professional who is keeping track of the skills they have developed and the areas they need to develop for their professional and career development this could be the most appropriate way to organise their portfolio. An example of this type of portfolio, in which the themes are skills based, will be demonstrated later in the chapter.

Assessment criteria

This might normally only be used in the context of students who are being assessed on particular areas of their course work. However, it can be used to demonstrate that one has achieved the requisite outcomes for membership of a professional body. For example, in the UK, the Chartered Institute of Library and Information Professionals[9] has a set of criteria for those applying for charted status within the organisation. These are:

1. ability to analyse and evaluate the effectiveness of the products/services/organisations referred to in the submission;

2. ability to identify and analyse problems encountered in practice;

3. competence in a range of management and professional skills developed through professional practice;

4. development of a personal professional viewpoint which is constantly re-assessed in the light of increasing experience and knowledge;

5. critical evaluation of personal performance and development;

6. analysis of personal learning outcomes from training received;

7. continuing professional development through reading, participation in professional affairs and attendance at courses/conferences;

8. understanding of the legal and regulatory framework of information and library provision in the UK;

9. an increased level of understanding of the relationship between theory and practice;

10. professional judgment through selection and presentation of material in the application.

The individual might choose to divide their portfolio for submission to the professional body in this way to ensure that they address the requirements of the accreditation procedure.

Indexing the portfolio

As already indicated, the portfolio needs to be indexed to enable the onlooker to easily access the information they are looking for. This information could be different for each person viewing the portfolio; hence the portfolio needs to be well indexed. Annotating the evidence is the first part of this process and including keywords on each piece will help the indexing process. If the evidence has keywords then a simple index using the keywords can be created and reference made to each piece that has that keyword associated with it. When creating an index one should try to bear in mind the questions that may be asked of the portfolio including:

- Where can I find information on this topic?
- Where can I find the feedback on this work?
- Where are the finished articles, projects etc.?

Other questions could, and should, be asked of the portfolio. Some of these will depend on the purpose of the portfolio, but it is important to keep these in mind so that the desired outcome is achieved.

The following reports on the development of a portfolio of statements to allow both students and practitioners in the information sector to chart their own personal and professional development within a clear framework of appropriate skills.

The key skills for information professionals portfolio

The Learning and Teaching Support Network, Centre for Information and Computer Sciences (LTSN-ICS)[10] based at Loughborough University in the UK is engaging with the Library and Information Science community to promote aspects of learning and teaching, including employability and skills development. The Centre has produced a portfolio to help with what the UK higher education community is calling personal development planning (PDP).

The portfolio adapted an existing method of recording skills to fit the needs of LIS professionals. This recording system is web-based and allows students to click on a skill, select the level that they have achieved and enter the evidence for that achievement within a form. It is currently used by construction management students, and was developed by the RAPID (Recording Academic, Professional and Individual Development)[11] team in the Civil and Building Engineering Department at Loughborough University and sanctioned by the Chartered Institute of Building in the UK. The team developed the RAPID Progress File as part of the DFEE-funded 'Recording Achievement in Construction Project' which ran from 1998–2000. Their work was highly successful and the team are now involved in RAPID 2000 'FDTL Project 34/99: Promoting Skill Development on Undergraduate Programmes in Civil and Building Engineering': a strategic approach based on professional development needs.

The skills that the RAPID Progress File asks students to acquire and reflect on were examined first. There are three distinct sets of skills: key skills, personal skills and professional skills. The areas described as key skills and personal skills are largely generic and as such needed little amendment to be of relevance to the library and information professional. However, the writing of a series of skills statements was required for the professional skills section for LIS. It is worth noting at this point that PDP is used to describe the benefits of using this portfolio. This is important as CPD may not be perceived in this way. Some employers, and some individuals, believe that CPD relates purely to the individual's professional role only. It could be argued that this is not constructive and that to be a competent information professional one must develop both personally and professionally.

The LTSN-ICS has defined and revised skills statements for the professional skills section of the portfolio for those working as LIS professionals. This required reviewing and combining LIS school course and module descriptions, the then Library Association and Institute of Information Scientists course accreditation guidelines[12] and also the QAA benchmarks.[13] The Information and Library Services National Occupational Standards[14] were also consulted as part of this process. After this process was completed these statements underwent review by members of the LIS community, including CILIP, academic departments and practitioners. This took place by holding focus groups and by inviting comments from participants. The process was iterative with the statements being reviewed by a focus group and individuals and then being rewritten at the LTSN-ICS until it was felt that a point had been reached where only piloting the document might reveal changes that should be made. At no stage of the process has it ever been considered that the statements were 'cast in stone' as they have undergone many amendments and may be altered further in the light of any future changes in the professional environment.

The Information and Library Science skills portfolio

Following these consultations a portfolio has been created that will enable both students and professionals to record and reflect upon their skills development. The portfolio is available in paper form and as a PDF document.[15]

It is structured into three sections, one each on key skills, personal skills and professional skills. Each of these sections contains a skills checklist at its head. Figure 3.1 shows the checklist for professional skills, but the complete listing of all three sections can be found in the PDF document.

The checklist is further divided into subsections and within each of these is a heading for the skill to be attained. Each skill has four levels of competence, which broadly speaking, are aligned as indicated in Table 3.1. However, there is a drawback to these levels that may not initially have been considered. Individuals may not be at undergraduate level when they begin their career in LIS, for example, they may have completed another degree and be undertaking a post-graduate qualification in LIS or they may have been working in an information environment in another capacity before starting a professional qualification. This would almost certainly mean that they have acquired some skills in professional and personal areas through employment and achieve high skills levels in the key skills area, particularly if

Figure 3.1   Professional skills checklist

SKILLS	A	B	C	D
INFORMATION RESOURCES				
Identification and Analysis				
Collection and Data Managment				
Knowledge Organisation, Recording and Retreival				
Evaluation				
INFORMATION SERVICE & ORGANISATION MANAGEMENT				
Strategic Management				
Financial Management and Planning				
Human Resource Management				
Service Assessment				
User Needs Analysis				
Development and Provision of Services				
Promotion				
User Education				
INFORMATION SYSTEMS				
Analysis and Design				
Implementation				
Evaluaton and Use				
Project Management				
POLICY, ENVIRONMENT AND SOCIETY				
Global Information Flow				
Information and Organisations				
Quality				
Professional Standards and Codes of Practice				
Regulation, Policies and Issues				

| Table 3.1 | Levels of competence |

Statement of Competence	Corresponding Level
Statement A	Start of Information and Library Science degree
Statement B	During Information and Library Science degree
Statement C	Completed Information and Library Science degree in first professional post
Statement D	Working towards chartered membership of professional body

they are already a graduate. Despite this drawback, if they are a novice in either recording skills or in the LIS field then the description of statement levels does help to give some context to their skills development.

In addition, there is also a substantial help section, with examples, at the front of the portfolio which provides support for the novice.

It is important to remember that the skill-set is not prescriptive, nor should it be, as no doubt many practitioners will be more skilled in some areas than others. Some will have achieved a level above D in some areas, while still acquiring skills from either the personal or key skill-set. This will depend largely on their current role within their organisation and their professional involvement.

Beyond the checklist there is a skill statement for each skill noted. The skills designated as identification and analysis within the section headed information resources is outlined in Figure 3.2. The user of the portfolio can see the stepped levels of progression from recognising the need for information at A, through more complex analysis of resources to level D where advanced search strategies are being utilised to meet information needs.

The user of the portfolio would tick the level they believe they have achieved and then quote the evidence in the

Figure 3.2 Information Resources – identification and analysis

INFORMATION RESOURCES

Identification and Analysis – Matching resources to enquiries

EVIDENCE OF YOUR DEVELOPMENT

	Please indicate your competence in this skill by ticking one of the four boxes	
A	I can recognise a need for information, identify appropriate resources to fit the need and begin to use simple techniques[1] to find the necessary information.[2]	
B	I can understand a user's enquiry for information, match the necessary resources with the information needed and by constructing a strategy[3] locate the required information. In doing this I recognise the need to gain relevant details from the enquirer and I understand access issues and how information from more than one source may be required.	
C	I can answer a complex user enquiry[4] by locating information using the appropriate search techniques with a clear knowledge of indexing and thesaurus construction. After accessing the necessary information I can analyse this and confirm that the information matches the need.	
D	I can successfully locate and access information to satisfy a complex user query, compare information from a variety of sources identified through the use of a range of search strategies, and ensure this clearly meets the information need. I can also apply this information to a problem and in keeping with copying and plagiarism requirements and best practice, organise and communicate the desired information appropriately.	

1. simple techniques: eg use library OPAC.
2. necessary information: print, audio visual, electronic journals, websites, multimedia images etc.
3. strategy: including using Boolean logic, phrase searching, truncation, etc.
4. complex user enquiry: search a range of information sources using a range of techniques.

What evidence do you have to support this?	Where is this evidence located?

bottom panels to show how they have achieved this. Evidence should be quoted if it adheres to the following guidelines previously noted above that it be valid, specific to the level, current, sufficient, authenticated, and documented.

It is unlikely that it is possible to do this for every level, but witness testimony and documentary evidence are the best support for any claims made by the individual.

In the light of evidence gathering, the individual is then able to plan their future activities towards attaining the next level of competence. To this extent the portfolio provides planning sheets that enable the user to review and reflect on their achievements to date and then set targets for their future professional development (see Figure 3.3).

Figure 3.3   Information Resources – planning future development

INFORMATION RESOURCES

Identification and Analysis – Matching resources to enquiries

PLANNING YOUR FUTURE DEVELOPMENT

Action Plan (Tasks to achieve my goal)	
Review, Reflection, Evaluation (Why do I need to achieve this?)	

This may seem a daunting task at the outset, but it is intended to be completed gradually so that the individual builds up a list of their skills and competencies which will enable them to build upon their professional competencies and identify their strengths and weaknesses. This is invaluable when building a CV and applying for jobs.

The portfolio has been piloted with both students and professionals with benchmarking questionnaires being used to determine their experiences to date regarding the monitoring of their personal development. Periodically further evaluation surveys were conducted to inform the pilot and determine whether the portfolio was achieving its aims by both being easy to understand and to complete.

This provides the widest possible feedback as to the portfolio's usefulness to those intent upon a career in the information and library sector. Evaluation carried out to date[16] indicates that there has been a significant increase in the ability of individuals to understand their skills development and in how to record that development.

The portfolio can be used to complement existing personal and professional development toolkits, such as CILIP's Turning Points Toolkit.[17] More than this, it should provide both recognition of the full range of skills that information and library professionals use in their work and enable individuals to compete effectively in the marketplace by being aware of the skills that they have developed through their own reflection. It will also enable individuals to analyse the skills they have and express their competencies to new and future employers.

Summary

Building portfolios has not, until the present moment, been an essential activity for information professionals. However, the changing environment requires that they be able to demonstrate their skills in many areas to both present and future employers. They might also be likely to present them as evidence for professional standards and status to a professional body. One of the best methods to do this is by creating and maintaining a portfolio that addresses the requisite areas for the individual concerned, remembering that for each individual the skill-set will be different depending on which aspect of information work they are involved with.

There are important factors that need to be foremost in the minds of information professionals when carrying out this activity. Of these, time and organisation are paramount. A portfolio is not an easy option, it is an effective way of gathering together evidence on our careers to date and cannot be completed overnight, no matter which option one takes. Therefore, the individual has to put aside enough time to make their portfolio work. In itself, this is insufficient, as the evidence to go in the portfolio is likely to be voluminous and one has to be sufficiently well organised so that the collected material is not overwhelming.

Implicit in the need to be organised is deciding on an appropriate structure for the portfolio. Different options can be made when making this decision, including time, pieces of work, topic or assessment criteria. Again, the portfolio should be created to suit the way in which the individual works. It is no small task to create a portfolio and any extra work will only be off-putting for the person trying to create it.

There are tools that can help the individual with planning the structure of the portfolio, some of which have been discussed. It should be stressed, however, that these tools are unlikely to fit every need that the individual may have, as such they should be used as a part of the process to build an effective record of professional development to date.

Selecting the right evidence is also crucial to the success of the portfolio. All evidence should be valid, reliable, sufficient, authentic and current. These judgments are to be made against the skills or competencies for which the professional is trying to provide evidence. Many types of evidence can be utilised in a portfolio, some of which are described earlier in the chapter, but the reader should not be restricted by this list, they are only suggestions and the reader should use whatever appears to be appropriate in their circumstances.

When planning the portfolio, close attention must be paid to the need for easy access to what could be quite a large selection of evidence. To ensure that this happens, the evidence must be appropriately annotated. To do this the evidence must be described in such a way that it is clear exactly what the evidence is; who created it; when it was created; why it was created, and what the evidence shows.

Indexing the portfolio is necessary to ensure that the evidence, as described in the above annotations, can be found by the observer, whether it be the individual themselves or an assessor. If appropriate keywords are used to describe the evidence then an index can link these keywords together with the evidence to allow topics, types of evidence or any other access point to be created.

Using these techniques, structures and tools can help the individual record their continuing professional development. It is not an easy task, especially if this is a new approach to recording professional development. Beginning a portfolio at the very beginning of a professional career, even as a student, will be easier as the evidence is not as voluminous as it may be at a later stage of a career. Adopting good habits at an early stage will make the task easier and more manageable. It will also provide valuable information for professional development.

Notes

1. P. Garrod and I. Sidgreaves (1997) *Skills for New Information Professionals: the SKIP Project*. London: Library Information Technology Centre.
2. Information Services National Training Organisation (2000) *Information and Library Services National Occupational Standards*. Bradford: ISNTO.
3. J. Feather (2003) Where have all the library schools gone. *Library and Information Update*. 2: 40–42.
4. Chartered Institute for Library and Information Professionals (1992) *The Framework for Continuing Professional Development*. London: Library Association.
5. S. Simosko (1991) *APL: A Practical Guide for Professionals*. London: Kogan Page.
6. W. Redman (1994) *Portfolios for Development: a Guide for Trainers and Managers*. London: Kogan Page.
7. Home Office (1984) *Data Protection Act*. London: HMSO.
8. D. Baume (2003) *Supporting Portfolio Development*. LTSN Generic Centre Continuing Professional Development Series No.3. York: Learning and Teaching Support Network.
9. Chartered Institute for Library and Information Professionals (2002) *Chartered Membership: Regulations and Notes of Guidance for Members Wishing to Apply for Chartered Membership of CILIP*. London: Chartered Institute for Library and Information Professionals.
10. Learning and Teaching Support Network – Centre for Information and Computer Sciences. Homepage: *http://www .ics.ltsn.ac.uk/* (visited 21 November 2003).
11. Loughborough University (2002) *RAPID 2000: Developing Professionalism, Competence and Excellence: http://rapid2k .lboro.ac.uk/* (visited 18 March 2003).
12. The Library Association and the Institute for Information Scientists (1999). *Joint Accreditation Instrument – Procedures for the Accreditation of Courses*. London: Library Association.
13. The Quality Assurance Agency for Higher Education. *Subject Benchmarking: http://www.qaa.ac.uk/revreps/subjrev/intro .htm.* (visited 17 September 2004).
14. Information Services National Training Organisation *op. cit.*

15. Learning and Teaching Support Network – Centre for Information and Computer Sciences. *Recording Skills Development for Information and Library Science: http:// www.ics.ltsn.ac.uk/resources/ilsresources.html* (visited 18 August 2003).

16. A. Brine and J. Feather (2003) Building a Skills Portfolio for the Information Professional. *New Library World*. 104 [1194/1195]: 455–463.

17. Centre for Research in Library and Information Management. *Turning Points, Moving into Management: A Learning Support Toolkit for the Continuing Professional Development of Library and Information Graduates: http://www.la-hq.org .uk/directory/training/turning.html* (visited 17 September 2004).

Programmes for development

Recording one's personal and professional development is important, as discussed in the previous chapters. The sooner the individual takes control of this aspect the more prepared they will be to take advantage of training and development opportunities. These can come in a variety of forms and at a variety of levels. This chapter will look at the possibilities and enable the reader to form their own judgment, if they were not already aware of the ways they could follow to maintain their professional competencies.

International

Some support is available at international level. The International Federation of Library Associations and Institutions (IFLA) is an umbrella organisation that supports libraries and librarians/information professionals across the world. They are especially concerned with developing the profession and to help level the playing field globally through providing support for the development of information and library services and professionals.

IFLA currently operates six core activities to support their aims. One of these is the Advancement of Librarianship Programme (ALP). This was launched in 1984 and has been fully operational since 1991. The ALP mission is:

to further the library profession, library institutions and library and information services in the developing countries of Africa, Asia and Oceania, and Latin America and the Caribbean. Within the special ALP areas the MTP goals are to assist in continuing education and training; to support the development of library associations; to promote the establishment and development of library and information services to the general public, including the promotion of literacy; and to introduce new technology into library services.[1]

This is an extremely wide remit, so IFLA works closely with relevant IFLA bodies and also with international and regional organisations to deliver a programme of carefully coordinated activities. Cooperation between these bodies and organisations includes fund raising, scholarships, attachment programmes, conferences, seminars, workshops, pilot projects, publications and databases. Many of these are not directed at the individual per se, but are intended to benefit the countries or regions where they have been implemented.

The priorities of the ALP are:

- library association development;
- human resources development;
- libraries and literacy;
- information technology in developing countries;
- information to the community with a special attention to indigenous communities.

It is the second of these, human resources development, which is aimed at individuals in the library and information profession. IFLA aims to develop library and information professionals by supporting projects for continuing education activities. This is carried out by holding seminars, workshops and in-service training. This could be in a variety of areas including information technology, and preservation and conservation methods.

To support professionals in what they describe as 'developing countries' IFLA offer the following:

- Harry Campbell IFLA Conference Attendance Grant;
- IFLA Travel Grant;
- Scholarships Asia and Oceania;
- Training attachments Asia and Oceania.

These enable travel and attendance at the IFLA conference from information professionals in these countries. They also offer scholarships to recognised programmes to develop individuals' skills and short training attachments within other services. Projects also enable the development of skills, for example, training packages have been developed in some countries to develop individuals on a local basis. Workshops and seminars have also been held including:

- networking of provincial and district libraries with mobile services into rural areas;
- policy development and management;
- information provision to rural communities;
- tools for library development;
- libraries for literacy in geographically and socially isolated communities.

Although IFLA's work largely tries to tackle the global information-rich and information-poor divide by offering opportunities to those countries needing to develop their libraries and professionals, it also provides development for all information professionals by bringing the community together from across the globe at the IFLA conference and satellite groups and sections.

Another international development programme is that of the Voluntary Service Overseas (VSO). This is a charity that uses volunteers to promote international development and 'bring people together to share skills, creativity and learning'.[2] It is the largest independent agency for sending volunteers across the globe. More than 29,000 volunteers have been sent to Africa, Asia, the Caribbean, the Pacific and Eastern Europe in response to requests for help. VSO has agencies in Canada, Kenya, the Netherlands and the Philippines, each of which recruits volunteers from across the globe. This approach of bringing together individuals from different cultures, enables the sharing of skills and learning for all those involved.[3]

Individuals have the opportunity to spend a year or more overseas working in countries without established library services. Projects may include building libraries or introducing services, such as literacy programmes. This benefits the country in which they are working and also provides them with an opportunity to develop their skills in an environment that demands both independence of spirit and the necessity of acquiring appropriate skills within a short timescale. Although volunteers are ostensibly sent out to help in countries because of the professional skill-set they already have, it is clear from VSO's website that these skills are considerably stretched and also that they have developed new skills that enhance their employability upon their return. This is due, in no small measure, to different cultures sharing and learning from one another.

These development programmes provide different experiences for professionals in different parts of the world. As with all things in life, it is the individual's outlook on life that will determine if these opportunities can help them develop their skills.

National

Many countries have a professional body for librarians and information workers, and avail themselves of the services that they offer. This may include relevant publications and training events. Many of them offer a form of development programme to promote and enhance the status of the information professional.

The Australian Library and Information Association (ALIA) states that CPD is a significant part of learning and should help:

- 'maintain members technical knowledge, professional skills and competencies;
- assist them to remain flexible and adaptable; and
- provide reasonable assurance to the community that they are keeping themselves up-to-date'.[4]

To support the professional development of their members, ALIA have instituted a CPD scheme with which members have to achieve compliance. This is in line with many other professions around the world who insist that members keep their skills and competencies up-to-date, so that both the individual and the profession can claim that they have achieved a high standard of professionalism which makes them eminently employable.

The CPD scheme introduced by ALIA requires that individuals perform a minimum of 20 hours of professional development in any one year and that over a three year period this figure should rise to 80 hours. Members are not able to carry across hours from one year to the next (e.g. if only 10 hours were done the following year then they have not met the minimum requirements) although they do count towards the three year total.

ALIA provides a list of areas and activities to guide its members. These include the following generic areas:

- team relationship skills;
- effective communication;
- information technologies and systems skills;
- management skills;
- critical and creative thinking;
- evaluation skills;
- information literacy skills;
- professional ethical standards;
- life-long learning.

They also provide a list of library and information specific areas including:

- library and information services strategic development;
- library and information policies and environments;
- information services;
- information systems and technologies;
- resource acquisition and management;
- research, analysis and interpretation techniques;
- management of information services and personnel;
- information sources.

The scheme also requires that development is carried out in a minimum of two areas from both the generic and library and information specific areas. To clarify this for members

ALIA provide definitions of professional activities and examples of those activities. The type of evidence required to satisfy the requirements is also documented so that individuals have a clear idea of what is expected. Table 4.1 is an excerpt from a table on the ALIA website[5] clearly showing the types of activity acceptable for CPD and how one would undertake that activity, by looking at the

Table 4.1 Suitable ALIA continuing professional development activities

Activity type	Definition	Examples	Evidence
Professional reading	As professional journals and magazines comprise a mix of both generic and LIS. Specific items, it is for the individual to decide to what extent reading a particular item constitutes CPD. Mere subscription to a publication does not constitute CPD. A recorded benefit must be derived from professional reading.	Professional journals Books/articles Business press Financial press Internet/electronic documents Pre-training course study	Record signed by supervisor or mentor
Formal education and training	This includes formal face-to-face education, individual study programmes and distance education that requires some evidence of completion.	Further qualifications Distance learning	Certificate
Informal learning activities	This includes any form of learning where there is no assessment.	Self-paced learning Audio/video tapes, CD-ROM Television programmes Distance learning Mentee in ALIA mentoring programme	Record signed by supervisor/ mentor

Table 4.1 **Suitable ALIA continuing professional development activities (cont'd)**

Activity type	Definition	Examples	Evidence
Presentations and papers	This includes the preparation and presentation of lectures, courses and discussion group papers of a technical nature (delivery only counted once).	In-house presentations Workshops Conferences Seminars	Conference programmes
Publications	Articles in professional journals, monographs, industry publications, training publications that are of a technical nature. This includes preparation time (publication only counted once for each article).	Refereed articles Non-refereed articles	Referee's report Citations
Attendance at conferences and meetings	This includes formal participation in such events as seminars, conferences and exhibitions as an observer.	Seminars Conferences Exhibitions	Receipt for conference Registration fees Signature of supervisor Conference delegate list
Association activities	Formal participation in ALIA activities, either by election or by invitation.	Committee work Group activities Elected rep. of ALIA meetings Mentor in ALIA mentoring programme	
Workplace learning	On the job learning activities where a recorded benefit is derived from participation.	In-house briefings In-house workshops/ seminars Structured training	Record signed by supervisor

examples column, and how that activity should be recorded by gathering evidence to supply to the professional body.

Activities are also subjected to a weighting system which ALIA have added to determine the benefit gained from each activity. This means that the time spent on an activity is multiplied by a weighting factor to give *CPD hours*. For example, professional reading has a weighting of 0.3, so to achieve ten hours of CPD reading activity, one has to read for 30 hours.

ALIA are extremely clear on those activities that are legitimately counted as continuing professional development. They are equally clear on those activities that do not constitute professional development. Within this category they include:

- normal working activities (except research);
- social activities (e.g. annual dinners);
- internal meetings (e.g. day-to-day staff meetings);
- general reading (e.g. newspapers).

This makes sense as you would not expect to include any activity as professional development. The emphasis for CPD should be on developing the individual's professional and transferable skills through legitimate channels, not as part of one's normal daily activities.

The process is documented through the use of an annual reporting sheet available from the ALIA website[6] that is submitted to the professional body. This is not a complex form and if the individual updates it on a regular basis then it should not be an onerous task. The ALIA version mentioned here could easily be adapted by the individual to create their own that would best fit their own circumstances.

Members are also expected to complete additional CPD audit sheets to record workplace learning and informal activities. These are not submitted but are retained by the individual to be produced on request. These audit record sheets, along with appropriate evidence, are required by ALIA as part of their audit process for the CPD scheme. Ten per cent of the members who have registered with the scheme, are contacted each year to provide evidence of their continuing development. This gives the scheme some credence with employers, as those members that are undertaking an audited scheme are proving that they are both professionally active and that their skills and knowledge are current. Employers who actively seek out those following continuous professional development, and support that same development, are making a conscious decision to invest in their staff. They are also protecting and enhancing their greatest asset. The One Umbrella Report recognises this and states: 'In a fast paced employment market, those with proven, up-to-date skills are able to take advantage of the most attractive job opportunities'.[7]

To support the process ALIA provide all members with a career development kit. The kit has been designed to assist members in their gathering of professional knowledge. It aims to:

- help individuals analyse their development needs;
- set objectives to address these needs;
- obtain input from managers, mentors and colleagues;
- maintain an appropriate record of professional development;
- assess development needs for the future.

The kit contains a workbook and worksheets that help the individual to assess:

- their primary goals and barriers to achieving them;
- the skills needed to achieve those goals;

- the level of skills required and whether they are needed in the short, medium or long term;
- which types of activity are necessary;
- the role of workplace learning in skills development;
- planning and recording of continuing professional development;
- building a portfolio;
- re-evaluating continuing professional development.

Using the kit is intended to help individuals meet the requirements for a sub-category of membership that, as previously discussed, proves the member's commitment and desire to develop their professional skills. It requires a considerable amount of time and form filling to achieve this level of professionalism. CPD schemes are recent additions to the professional's armoury and as such, will develop until they settle at an appropriate level of auditing combined with professional development activities.

This type of scheme is new to the profession and is becoming more prevalent. In the UK the professional body, CILIP, is beginning its own CPD scheme. This is imperative as there is a need to prove to employers, in an increasingly competitive market, that members of the library and information profession are eminently employable and are an asset to the employing organisation.

It should be noted at this stage that anyone who has created and maintained their own portfolio, as described in Chapter 3, to record their continuing professional development will be able to adapt, with little difficulty, to a CPD scheme. They will have already obtained the skills in the collection and collation of evidence and the subsequent referencing of the material enabling it to be accessed quickly on future occasions.

Individuals may find difficulty in undertaking some professional development activities. In some instances employers may not be in a position to offer access to paid courses or may place limits on the activities of their employees. In subsequent chapters some methods for accessing professional development activities will be discussed to aid the individual in finding alternative sources for development.

Sector-wide

There are also sector-wide organisations that support professionals in different spheres of the library and information profession. Sector can be used to describe anything that constitutes a definable subset of the information profession, such as government or medical libraries.

The Association of College and Research Libraries (ACRL) is 'the professional organization for librarians and other information specialist in academic and research institutions throughout the world'.[8] Located in the USA, it is a slight exaggeration to claim that it is global, especially as other countries have similar bodies, such as the University, College and Research Group in the UK. These bodies do have good links with the main professional body in the country; in the case of the ACRL it is the American Library Association (ALA).

The ACRL Statement on Professional Development makes it transparent that it is the responsibility of the individual to 'raise the bar against which ACRL members and staff measure their commitment to professional excellence through continued learning'.[9] It goes beyond this to state that professional development is a shared responsibility and a partnership between the individual, graduate schools of library and information science and employers. Each partner has an important role to play in promoting and sustaining professional development, but it does hinge on a commitment by the individual for personal growth.

The ACRL reviews the context in which librarians and information professionals are required to develop their skills and, in the statement, lay down the responsibilities of the partners previously mentioned.

The ACRL states that the individual must:

- identify the personal and professional skills and knowledge necessary for present and future needs;
- continuously assess their skills and knowledge;
- use the above processes to develop a personal learning strategy.

These are all familiar comments that have been made in the previous chapters, but they do suggest that there are partners who can help, for example, the National Research Council's (NRC) Committee on Information Technology Literacy. They have analysed the complex set of skills and knowledge which constitute this area into a taxonomy made of three groupings to provide a definition for an individual's fluency in information technology skills[10] as shown in Table 4.2.

Academic librarians should then share their skills with colleagues, through writing, mentoring or other methods, and by continuously articulating their professional development needs to their employer and their professional body.

Responsibilities are also laid down by the ACRL for the other partners involved in the process. The ACRL are expected to provide:

Table 4.2   NRC's components of fluency in information technology

Intellectual capabilities	Engage in sustained reasoning Manage complexity Test a solution Manage problems in faulty solutions Organise and navigate information structures and evaluate information Collaborate Communicate to other audiences Expect the unexpected Anticipate changing technologies Think about information technology abstractly
Foundational concepts	Computers Information systems Networks Digital representation of information Information organisation Modelling and abstraction Algorithmic thinking and programming Universality Limitations of information technology Societal impact of information and IT
Contemporary skills	Setting up a personal computer Using basic operating system features Using a word processor to create a text document Using a graphics and/or artwork package to create illustrations, slides or other image based expressions of ideas Connecting a computer to a network Using the Internet to find information and resources Using a computer to communicate with others Using a spreadsheet to model simple processes or financial tables Using a database system to set up and access useful information Using instructional materials to learn how to use new applications or features

- help in identifying and participating in professional development programmes;

- facilitating personal approaches to learning, e.g. seminars, meetings and publications;

- assessment tools for evaluating skills and competencies;

- promoting collaborative learning with partners.

Library and information science schools are expected to foster this process at an early stage by promoting the individual's own analysis of their learning styles and the necessity for continuing professional development. Employing institutions should show their commitment to their staff development through financial support, time off for study or through other means, as it is to their benefit as a team that is composed of highly-skilled staff will provide a high level of service to users.

Similarly in the UK the British and Irish Association of Law Librarians (BIALL) provide a focus for the development of the individual within the legal sector. Although they do not provide programmes for development and recording mechanisms, in the same way that the larger professional bodies can (e.g. CILIP and ALIA) they do ensure that individuals working within that sector have access to continuing professional development. On payment of a membership fee the individual is entitled to:

- a subscription to 'legal information management' journal;

- the BIALL newsletter;

- website, with member only areas;

- conference discounts and bursaries;

- professional development course discounts;

- BIALL publication discounts;

- BIALL annual salary survey;
- discounts on related publications.

Many of these services are offered by similar bodies, but the most important information to be gleaned from this is that there are many bodies in sectors that offer support for different forms of professional development for the individual. These are all accessible, (sometimes with the necessary payment of a membership fee, of which only so many can be usefully acquired), but to be effective, it is the individual's personal responsibility to direct their learning and pursue those options that will develop their skills and knowledge. Nobody else is in a better position to know their strengths and weaknesses and how they wish to develop their career, but the drive must come from the individual. There are always external driving forces, usually within the employing organisation, but the individual is responsible for themselves and their professional image. Those that do not want to develop will, at best, stay where they are and, at worst find themselves possibly with no job after an organisational restructuring.

Similar organisations exist in the health sciences sector. In the UK, the Health Libraries Group, is under the umbrella of the parent organisation CILIP. They provide professional development activities for their members. In the USA the Medical Library Association (MLA) provides support for individuals operating in this sector. Like BIALL in the UK they provide a similar list of resources that can be utilised for professional development including:[11]

- the *Journal of the Medical Library Association*;
- books and other MLA publications;
- continuing education courses that are credit bearing;

- scholarships;

- web-based and distance learning opportunities;

- information on local continuing education provision.

They provide ample opportunity for those in the sector to develop their skills at both a national and local level. The latter is of more importance in larger countries; in countries such as the UK, travelling distances are not so much of a factor as, for example, in the USA, where it could take a long while to travel to an event. This could in itself become a barrier to learning. With the availability of distance learning programmes, however, the MLA goes some way to overcoming this obstacle.

Regional

Most national bodies have regional structures that can provide support for information professionals. In the USA the structure of the ALA includes 'chapters' spread throughout the country, examples of which include:

- West Virginia Library Association;

- Mississippi Library Association;

- Maryland Library Association;

- Texas Library Association;

- Oregon Library Association.

These are important support mechanisms for members and can be for non-members. If the individual is not a member then they are largely unaware of the majority of the activities that a professional association can, and does provide. The individual should seriously consider becoming a member, if not for professional qualifications, then for the professional support that it offers. The ALA chapters consider increasing their membership a priority. To help achieve this end in 1999–2000 the ALA Chapter Relations Committee carried out a survey to determine the best practices used from state to state in the USA. The results of the survey are available on the ALA website[12] and although it looks at how to attain new members, it also reviews how to retain them. The ALA found that some of the best ways to retain members is by supporting their professional development by:

- creating mentor programmes;
- offering loans and scholarships;
- reducing rates for conferences and programmes;
- strong publications programme;
- providing means for members to talk to each other, such as online discussion groups.

Chapter websites provide users with the information they need to take advantage of these benefits. The New York Library Association website[13] emphasises its annual conference and continuing education, while that of the Colorado Library Association[14] offers discounts on publications and workshops. There are many similar benefits across the ALA chapters that can be helpful to information professionals.

Similar groups exist in other countries. In the UK, CILIP has a regional structure of branches that provide support in those areas. Berks, Bucks and Oxon is the branch that supports members in the counties of Berkshire, Buckinghamshire and Oxford, holding meetings and providing facilities to enable members to revalidate their professional development with the national body. This latter responsibility is part of a new focus for the professional body to promote library and information workers in the regions to employers, thus promoting the profession as a whole and the quality and level of its member's skills. A new London branch was inaugurated in 2004 to support the UK capital. Previously, London belonged to a larger branch, but with the city's size and transport links, it made more sense to have a London branch to stand on its own and provide the support that other branches provide.

Special interest groups may also have regional structures, if their membership is large enough, to deliver training and support. The Career Development Group (CDG) and Personnel, Training and Education Group (PTEG) provide workshops in the regions, but most specifically they provide two networks for the professional body that supports continuing professional development. The CDG operates the Registration Liaison Officer (RLO) network which runs courses and offers advice for candidates who have registered for Chartership with CILIP. Similarly PTEG operates the Supervisor Liaison Officer (SLO) which runs training and advice for supervisors of the previously mentioned Chartership candidates. This is invaluable as professionals who have already achieved Chartership and who are committed to professional development freely give their time to help enhance the skills of the newer entrants to the profession.

Conversely there are also regional groups that have special interest sections. The Illinois Library Association Resources and Technical Services Forum Technology User Group[15] provides a means for those that work in technical areas in libraries, such as systems librarians, to network and share experiences as a means of support. This is another invaluable tool to keeping abreast of current developments in the field.

In the UK there is a consortium known as East Midlands Academic Libraries in Cooperation (EMALINK), which provides joint training activities in the East Midlands region for academic librarians. The consortium provides free events for those wishing to attend by virtue of each library arranging and hosting one event during the year. Eleven institutions belong to the consortium, so all staff have the chance to attend events aiming to 'network and build contacts with staff doing a similar job in other local academic libraries'.[16] Consequently informal contact can follow beyond the events' close.

Local

It is difficult to determine where regional support might be clearly delineated from local. At a more local level, however, support can be found from the employing organisation, consortia, or other professional groups in the vicinity.

The employing organisation will usually have schemes that can be used to support professional development, although they may often not be perceived as such. These can include:

- staff development review;
- appraisal schemes;
- performance review;
- mentoring;
- staff development schemes.

These will differ from organisation to organisation, but in general they offer the individual a means to access training specific to their needs. Staff development reviews are used in the public sector in the UK. This is an annual process where the objectives of the organisation are used during an individual's annual review to determine whether any new skills will be required in the coming year to meet the needs of the service. These may also attempt to look ahead at the development of the individual and prepare them for future roles within the organisation, possibly in a supervisory capacity or maybe the development of IT skills.

Appraisal schemes may follow similar activities but place more emphasis on the achievements of the previous year to actually determine if the individual has developed during that time. Most professionals are extremely conscientious and have achieved the expected objectives for the year. The individual, however, may still be wary of the process, but it can be a good method to access training and development by the individual if handled appropriately. Performance reviews place more emphasis on the achievements of the individual over the previous year. Again most professionals achieve their objectives to a greater or lesser degree. For the individual this is an opportunity to bolster their skills and gain access to training for the next review period to enable them to develop. Further training can be argued to be necessary if targets have not been achieved during the period if some vital training was necessary and not provided. Equally if there are forthcoming changes in the individual's environment that are known, then training can be prepared for these. An example of this might be where legislative changes are due to come into force and the library or information service needs to prepare its staff for these changes.

One's colleagues and peers are also an invaluable resource for professional development. They can provide a number of useful services for the professional. The most important aspect of using one's peers as a resource is the fact that they provide an effective sounding board for ideas for training and development. They are often keen to develop themselves and exchanging ideas for training or for sources to access relevant training materials with other colleagues benefits everyone, including the employing organisation. Colleagues can also be useful as mentors for the individual. Some are experienced professionals and can provide invaluable insights into both the employing organisation and the professional world. Some organisations and some professional bodies do provide mentoring schemes to support the individual, often this is the line manager within the organisation, but sometimes this is not appropriate and a mentor from another organisation would be preferred, although this will often depend on the individual set of circumstances. Further discussions on mentoring will occur in the following chapter.

Staff development schemes are more common in employing organisations in the current climate. Employers are aware that their staff are their most valuable asset and consequently put their resources into developing their own personnel. This provides benefits for the individual in the form of readily accessible training and development. In a British Library Research and Development Report[17] Sylvia Webb reviewed continuing professional development in professional firms. Of the 65 participating firms, 50 provided internal courses and 60 supported attendance on external courses including payment of fees. Many of these firms would have training programmes based on the firm's major discipline, for example law or accountancy. Despite this the development programme often contained many generic training packages of use to the library and information professional including:

- IT;
- presentation skills;

- legal issues;
- finance;
- marketing;
- supervisory skills.

Many firms offer support for their staff and it is worth investigating what is available, if anything, and how to access the training. Even more encouraging is that this study also revealed that 29 firms provided actual library and information training programmes. This is not uncommon in firms that recognise the value of their LIS staff. The provision of training for staff becomes harder with smaller firms as the margins of the business can restrict their ability to invest in their employees' training needs. There are, however, other ways in which staff can develop their skills even if their employer does not or cannot provide help. The individual can draw upon the suggestions made in the following chapter.

Consortia may exist at a local level that the individual could use to facilitate their professional development. In the UK, the Libraries Agreement in Leicestershire, Leicester and Rutland (LAILLAR) body links the public and academic libraries in the area; in neighbouring Derbyshire, the Derbyshire Information Group (DIG) is a similar group. They enable joint visiting between libraries to share good practice and exchange views. They also provide staff training sessions to encourage a greater awareness of the range and variety of services on offer.[18] Many local bodies will exist across the globe, and almost all will be invisible to the outside world except to the individual working within that community. Individuals will need to investigate for themselves what may be available in their vicinity.

Summary

The development of the individual depends on their own ability to determine their needs and gain access to the relevant training. Many training programmes can be accessed to support individuals in their quest for development, no matter where they are in the world.

Internationally, organisations such as IFLA provide support for those regions of the world where the library services are developing, as are the professional associations and library and information professionals within those countries. However, despite the help on offer it remains to be seen how much impact this has within these areas, although one would like to think that real change is taking place.

Professional associations operating at a national level provide continuing professional development for their members through different methods. Some provide CPD schemes that ensure both quality and quantity of professional training, while many provide training courses and methods for the sharing and dissemination of good practice.

Sector specific bodies at a national level provide more relevant training for professionals who work in areas where there are distinct needs for information professionals, such as the academic or legal sectors. Membership of these bodies can be as important as membership of the foremost professional body in the country itself.

One of the strongest support mechanisms for the individual is to be found at regional and local levels. There are likely to be more opportunities to attend local training sessions and to network with library and information professionals in the same area. Creating and maintaining ties with other professionals ensures that the individual is not working in a vacuum and that they receive support from their peers to receive a wider appreciation of the issues within the profession.

Notes

1. International Federation of Library Associations and Institutions. *IFLA's Core Activity for the Advancement of Librarianship Programme (ALP): http://www.ifla.org/VI/1/alp.htm* (visited 19 March 2004).
2. Voluntary Services Overseas. *What is VSO?: http://www.vso.org.uk/whatis/index.htm* (visited 22 March 2004).
3. Voluntary Services Overseas Canada. *VSO's International programs: http://www.vsocanada.org/* (visited 22 March 2004).
4. Australian Library and Information Association. *Continuing Professional Development. http://www.alia.org.au/education/cpd/index.html* (visited 27 January 2004).
5. Australian Library and Information Association. *Continuing Professional Development. http://www.alia.org.au/education/cpd/activities.html* (visited 18 March 2004).
6. Australian Library and Information Association. *Continuing Professional Development. http://www.alia.org.au/education/cpd/record.sheets.html* (visited 24 September 2004).
7. The One Umbrella Team (2001) Continuing Professional Development Update. *TOUR: The One Umbrella Report*, 2(1): *http://www.oneumbrella.com.au* (visited 15 March 2004).
8. Association of College and Research Libraries. *ACRL Statement on Staff Development: http://www.ala.org/ala/acrl/acrlpubs/whitepapers/acrlstatement.htm* (visited 23 March 2004).
9. Ibid.
10. National Research Council's Commission on Physical Sciences, Mathematics and Applications. *Being Fluent with Information Technology: http://www.nap.edu/books/030906399X/html/index.html* (visited 15 April 2004).
11. Medical Library Association. *MLANET: Education: http://www.mlanet.org/education/index.html* (visited 23 March 2004).

12. American Library Association. *Membership Best Practices: http://www.ala.org/* (visited 23 March 2004).
13. New York Library Association. *Homepage: http://www.nyla .org/nylaweb1.htm* (visited 23 March 2004).
14. Colorado Library Association. *Homepage: http://www .cla-web.org/benefits.htm* (visited 23 March 2004).
15. Yahoo. *Yahoo Groups: ilartsftech: http://groups.yahoo.com/ group/ilartsftech/* (visited 27 September 2004).
16. East Midlands Academic Libraries in Co-operation (2003) *EMALINK: focusing on staff development and training.* Leicestershire: EMALINK (pamphlet).
17. S.P. Webb (1991) *Best Practice: Continuing Professional Development for Library/Information Staff in UK Professional Firms.* British Library R & D Report 6039. Berkhamsted: Sylvia P Webb; pp. 11–17.
18. Libraries Agreement in Leicestershire, Leicester and Rutland (2002) *Developing Access to Libraries in Leicestershire and Rutland.* Leicestershire: LAILLAR.

5

Support for the developing information professional

What kinds of support are available for those who want to develop their skills? The previous chapter reviewed how professional associations and groups provide continuing professional development opportunities for the individual across local, national and international boundaries. Professional groups are ostensibly networks, or networking opportunities, that the information professional can use to their advantage. Most require some form of membership, and usually the payment of a fee, to enable the individual to benefit from the community concerned.

Networks

There are other forms of networking that do not revolve around professional membership, which can be investigated by the individual. These include the following:

- personal contacts;
- colleagues;
- courses;
- discussion groups;

- weblogs;
- newsfeeds and RSS.

Personal contacts

The individual can cultivate their own set of personal contacts through their professional development activities. It does not hurt to ask a question of another professional at an event or exhibition that may help in the individual's personal or professional development. Indeed, many are happy to help a fellow professional; the library profession is known for its ability to collaborate, to provide services and share resources; professionals are usually willing to give advice and help no matter how exalted their standing in the library and information community.

Over time, all individuals will come into contact with others sharing similar interests and these contacts should be cultivated; information should be shared with them thus creating a community with common interests. This will lead to the individual developing their own informal network which they can use to support themselves in their professional work. It is also possible that this may lead to the individual discovering a mentor to guide them in their professional development. (Further discussion on mentoring is to be found later in this chapter.)

Colleagues

Workplace colleagues are a good source of information. It takes many years to learn the intricacies of the organisation within which one is working. Reliance on colleagues will be of importance if the individual wishes to deliver a competent service and more importantly to develop and improve that service. Colleagues are a valuable source of information on which internal courses one should attend, who is the best person to contact regarding particular aspects of work and how to tackle the acquisition of particular new skills. Many of them will belong to professional organisations and will be able to show the appropriate ways that a professional association can help the individual develop their skills and keep developing them throughout their career. To a new employee, colleagues will offer the best source of information to become competent and confident within their new working environment.

Courses

Attendance at workshops, seminars and courses will benefit the individual. There are various types of course that are available for the individual to attend. Chapter 2 has briefly reviewed the options available, but it is worth revisiting some of these. There are many variations of course format that one can undertake, which can include:

- computer-assisted learning aids (e.g. CD-based tutorials);
- e-learning (such as that provided through VLEs);
- open (or flexible) learning;
- exhibitions;
- internal courses;
- external courses;
- seminars;
- workshops;
- focus groups.

As can be seen from the list there are many headings that one would not immediately consider a course, but as a method of professional development they are all equally valid.

Computer-assisted learning aids come in many formats and might include an online tutorial and test, such as the European Computer Driving Licence (ECDL),[1] or even a CD that might come as a support tool in a self-help manual; there is an abundance of the latter available for information technology applications. Some of these may incur a cost to the individual to obtain, but others are available from the library or from free sources, such as Techtutorials.[2]

E-learning is used in a wider context than computer-based learning. Many institutions are moving to the use of VLEs including Blackboard[3] and WebCT.[4] This enables the learner to access materials remotely to the institution delivering the course, thus making it more conducive to part-time learners who can access material from home. With a greater number of electronic resources available from a computer desktop, through secure mechanisms such as Athens,[5] more control is being given to the individual to work when they are able.

Closely related to e-learning, and currently almost indistinguishable, is open or flexible learning. Open learning has always been available from providers such as the Open University[6] in the UK, with the provision of course packs that individuals use to study at a distance to acquire new skills. Many courses are now being delivered online, thus blurring the boundaries between the methods of delivery. However, the overriding concern for the individual is that they have control of when they study. They are able to build study time into their work and personal schedules, irrespective of whether the study material is available online or in the form of a hardcopy course pack.

Exhibitions are always valuable and can enlighten the individual as to the benefits or drawbacks to current applications that might enhance their library or information service. Individuals can usually attend these free of charge and can gain valuable insight into the current trends within the sector (for example, a library management system, where a demonstration and queries session regarding its capabilities would help the individual determine whether it had any place in their service). This can also apply to shelving, furniture or any other aspect of service provision.

Internal courses are often found within most organisations. The larger the organisation the more varied the programme can be. These may range from courses on project management, through supervisory skills to health and safety. These courses are highly valuable for a number of reasons. First, they allow the individual to develop their skills in a manner relevant to their own organisation, where the training is more likely to be geared to their own working environment. Second, they cover a broad range of skills that will be pertinent to their own particular job, but will also allow them to develop skills for future roles within the organisation. Attending courses that allow the development of skills for managing others will help prepare the individual to take advantage of opportunities as they arise within the organisation. Finally, they are usually provided at no cost to the individual and as such are invaluable.

External courses are not dissimilar to internal courses, but do have, in most cases, financial implications for either the individual or their employer, before they can attend. However, they are often organised by professional associations, or similar bodies, that draw upon the local, or national (and sometimes international), expertise that is available to hold the event. This will boost the confidence of the attendee (and of the employer who is paying), in the belief that they have the benefit of the most current 'thinking' and/or training available. Courses of this nature will always require advance booking to guarantee a place. Planning which skills and courses the individual requires, is essential for this type of course.

The range of courses includes workshops, where the delegates are actively involved in the event, and seminars where the onus will be on the presentation of information to the participants. Workshops allow more practical training to be given, with those attending being invited to try some things for themselves and to give their own opinions. The individual's own learning style will dictate which will be of the greatest benefit to them.

Courses of a much longer duration should be considered. Attending an institution that provides relevant degree courses will give recognised professional development. The MBA, for example, would develop the necessary skills for working at a managerial level within an organisation. Other courses offered by library schools across the globe might include IT-based skills, or those skills related to particular areas of specialisation, such as children's librarianship or the health sector.

Lastly, there are focus groups, which are more interactive than some of the other methods discussed above. These are valuable because they focus on specific aspects of library and information work and the individual is also fully expected to participate. The emphasis is on sharing experience so that everyone who attends can take something away from the event and try different or innovative approaches in their own workplace.

Discussion groups

Discussion groups are extensively used in the library and information community. They provide an access point for like-minded individuals to come together as a community via electronic means. Often organised around specific interests or disciplines, discussion groups allow individuals to share their concerns on particular issues and also provide solutions for others who are looking for inspiration.

Anderson and Kanuka[7] suggest that online groups provide the following:

- no limitations on time;
- ability to reflect before taking part;
- capability for research;
- communication on a global scale.

These points are clear; users can join in with online groups whenever they feel it is appropriate and can think about their contribution before they make themselves known to the online forum. The list and its associated archive can also aid the individual's research as they can search the archive to see if information is available on a topic that interests them, and if not, they can pose a question to the forum. It also gives the ability to discuss issues with individuals across the globe and in locations that are remote from their own workplace.

There are subtle differences between some online forums. Bernier and Bowen[8] state that the different forums are:

- bulletin board systems;
- mailing lists;
- newsgroups;
- web forums.

Bulletin board systems allow users to send e-mail, join discussion lists, download files and access news items. WOWbb[9] illustrates a number of the features attributed to bulletin boards.

Mailing lists are discussion groups that take place through the mechanism of a mass e-mail distribution system. After subscribing to the list individuals are able to post messages to the list and are able to receive responses to aid them with their query. Some lists are moderated and controlled by some groups to ensure that only known individuals can take part. Two of the most well known examples are Listserv[10] and Majordomo.[11] Most professional groups also have a number of lists that individuals can join. The American Library Association has many discussion groups including Community Information and Referral and Middle Management.[12] Mailing lists are popular because they are easy to use and e-mail has become a standard form of communication for many.

Newsgroups are different from lists in that they provide an arena where messages are simply posted by individuals. They are not moderated and are used by large groups, for example, the public newsgroup provided by Google.[13] These are useful but require more effort to find the required information, due to the large number of postings made to the groups.

Web forums are a current development and use dynamic web interfaces to make the content of discussions available. Using an underlying database, messages are more accessible through the presentation of related links and can be searched by the user. These media are still developing and are allowing better access to mailing lists and newsgroups. Further online developments are taking place (and will continue to do so as the technology changes) some of which are discussed in the next section.

Weblogs

Commonly known as *blogs*, a weblog is a 'website that contains brief entries arranged in chronological order'.[14] Using free software such as Blogger,[15] individuals are able to create a weblog. Individuals can subscribe to many weblogs to keep up-to-date with activities in a particular field. Equally, they might like to create their own, to provide information for others in a particular area. This would help inform others and would require the individual to keep the weblog up-to-date, thus ensuring one's own knowledge is current.

This may sound simple, but remember that it does take a considerable amount of time to maintain a weblog, not just in creating it, but in keeping abreast of new developments; making the site easier for users to search; getting feedback to develop the format; ensuring that more users visit the site by sending out newsletters and developing feeds from and to other websites.

There are numerous weblogs available in the community, but it is worth seeking those genuine nuggets of good information, most often produced by those with a reputation in their field. Weblogs usually have an archive and enable visitors to make their own comments about entries that have been posted. A useful source of weblogs related to library and information work worldwide can be found at LibDex, the library index.[16]

Newsfeeds and RSS

Accessing weblogs can be simplified by bookmarking them, as with any website, but as there are so many it is more efficient to monitor them via a newsfeed. Newsfeeds are 'services that use RSS to allow you to receive, within one page, many of these sources'.[17] RSS (Rich Site Summary) uses extensible mark-up language (XML) to extract headlines or content to be incorporated into other websites. Many library websites now take newsfeeds from the BBC in the UK. Individuals with specialist interests have created most weblogs and newsfeeds, but the increasing usage of weblogs and newsfeeds should see more information services adopting them to promote their services. It is worth seeking them out and reviewing their application in one's own working environment.

Mentoring

The process of mentoring has been utilised for centuries. Traditionally the relationship between master and apprentice was the mentoring process at its most productive. The experienced master would train and develop the skills of the apprentice so that these skills would be carried forward to future generations. Mentoring has changed considerably over the years, but the concept remains the same: skills and knowledge are passed on from one experienced individual to someone who is less experienced.

What is mentoring?

Mentoring has been defined by many authors, but does not conform to any short concise definition in any literature, in any country. Interestingly there is also no single definition that is applied to formal or informal schemes across the globe. The term *mentee* is preferred here, in place of mentoree or protégé as used by some writers on the topic.

An interesting development is the differentiation between the US approach, and that taken by Europe, Australia and New Zealand. Although no approach to mentoring should be ruled out, the US schemes place more emphasis on the relationship between mentor and mentee, suggesting an emotional bond between the two, akin to a 'mixture of parent and peer'.[18] The literature further emphasises a sponsorship and a more hands-on role in the USA. This is different from the European Mentoring Centre definition, described by Clutterbuck as 'offline help by one person to another in making significant transitions in knowledge, work or thinking'.[19]

The European model encourages individuals to develop themselves and is used because it is thought that if an individual is closely linked to their mentor, (e.g. a line manager) it is harder to be open and honest. It is also more common that mentors are not necessarily higher in the hierarchy, but are, as already mentioned above, more experienced. As a consequence they may be peers or even juniors in some areas of expertise, especially IT.

Eric Parsloe states that the process is intended, 'to help and support people to manage their own learning in order to maximise their potential, develop their skills, improve their performance, and become the person they want to be'.[20] This definition complements the ethos of continuing professional development. It is the responsibility of the individual to develop their skills and competencies, using any means at their disposal. Mentoring can be one of the most productive methods of achieving this, if the mentor and mentee relationship is appropriately managed by all those involved.

The fields of mentoring and coaching are expanding, but it is also clear that approaches are different across the globe, with different organisations trying to capture the 'essence of mentoring'. This is unlikely to be achieved as it is a very personal experience for both mentor and mentee, which will differ from person to person; from organisation to organisation; from sector to sector; and from country to country. The fact that many organisations now operate on a global level will also mean that the individual may encounter either of the mentoring models, whether US or European.

The mentoring relationship

The relationship between the mentor and the mentee is complex and as a result care needs to be taken in nurturing it. Mentoring is a process based on the relationship between two people. Consequently the actions of each affect the benefits that the other receives from the process. Both mentor and mentee will have prior expectations which they bring to the relationship and will, through their own behaviour and actions, affect the benefits and the outcomes received by both parties. To make the process worthwhile, both the mentor and the mentee must receive some positive benefits as outcomes of the process. If they do not then the relationship between the two will collapse. To avoid this, both parties must manage their expectations and use the process, (e.g. number of meetings, methods used etc.), to support the development of the relationship.

Clutterbuck provides some useful (and simple) methods of viewing the mentoring relationship and helping the individual to learn. He describes two variables determining the relationship as:

- who is in charge?
- what are the individual's needs?

The first of these, relates to the tone of the relationship. Is the mentor controlling the direction of the process or, are they allowing the mentee to set the agenda? If the former, then the mentor will direct the individual towards very clearly defined career, or personal goals. The mentor will largely set the agenda for any meetings or discussions that they have and will give very strong, clear advice on how the mentee should take their development forward. In the latter this process will be almost the reverse. The mentee will be encouraged to set the agenda for discussions or meetings, set their own goals and decide on their own route forward. The mentor will advise and encourage them in these activities, but will be endeavouring to make them self-reliant. In the case of personal development Clutterbuck sees the second of these as the most beneficial to the individual, as it is making them more proactive in their own development.[21]

The second aspect relates to the individual's needs and how they might need to be nurtured or stretched to develop. Everyone will develop in different ways and across different periods of time. In this respect the mentor will need to provide different levels of support at different times. On some occasions they will need to nurture the individual and encourage them, while at other times it will be more appropriate to stretch or challenge them to enable them to develop their skills and achieve their goals.

Methods used to help the individual learn should be incorporated into the relationship. Clutterbuck[22] suggests that there are five styles that, combined with the relationship variables discussed above, will support the development of the individual. These are:

- coaching;
- counselling;
- networking;

- guiding;

- mentoring.

Coaching is described as a 'directive' method of helping someone, especially if its is something with which they are having difficulty, going so far as to even demonstrate the process or technique.

Counselling is a supportive process where the mentor listens to the individual and helps them to analyse their own decisions on how to develop their skills or career.

Networking is essential to developing the skills of the individual and helping them achieve their goals, whether in aiding them to discover what they need to know, or how to influence others, over whom they may not have direct control. The mentor will help direct them to appropriate sources and may make introductions or encourage them to make their own.

Guiding is a more direct approach for mentors and often requires giving advice to the mentee. Encouraging the individual to reflect on their experiences does help them to develop, but sometimes it is more appropriate to advise the individual, pointing out where they have gone wrong. It will always be a balancing act for the mentor who must decide on whether direct advice is better than getting the mentee to reflect on an experience.

Lastly mentoring is actually an amalgam of the other four. It draws on the other styles and a good mentor will use them all, at different times and in different circumstances to provide the individual with the best mentoring experience.

Phases of the relationship

The relationship between mentor and mentee is not an endless process. It will have a beginning, an end and phases in between. As the individual progresses through their career and develops their skills, then eventually they will outgrow their mentor and will need to look to others or take full control of their own development themselves.

The phases, as suggested by the Empathy Project,[23] are:

- initiation;
- goal setting;
- developmental learning;
- winding down;
- dissolving.

The first of these is obviously the stage at which the two parties get to know each other and build a bond between each other. Then they will devise goals and plan on how the individual will achieve these. The third phase, developmental, requires the two working together to enable the mentee to develop their skills and knowledge. After achieving their objectives there will eventually be a winding down of the relationship where the process is evaluated and reviewed before the mentoring relationship is discontinued. A professional relationship will, however, exist beyond this.

The mentor

Different authors have produced different definitions of what a mentor may be, including primary and secondary mentors. It is clear, however, that there can be only one primary or main mentor. Although an individual can have many partial mentors who may advise on aspects of their career or development, only one can be the primary and they will usually be a more senior figure in the organisation's hierarchy. This is important as their seniority will give them the ability and appropriate levels of experience to support the individual and introduce them to other people and experiences within the organisation. Eric Parsloe quotes a report by the Council for National Academic Awards (CNAA) and the Government Training Agency, 'high quality mentoring is concerned with competence, experience and clear role-definition, but it also crucially depends upon the right balance of personal qualities'.[24] The same report stated that a good mentor would characteristically have the following attributes:

- 'good motivators, perceptive, able to support the objectives of the programme and fulfil their responsibilities to the candidate;

- high performers, secure in their own position within the organisation and unlikely to feel threatened by, or resentful of, the candidate's opportunities;

- able to show that a responsibility for mentoring is part of their own job description;

- able to establish a good and professional relationship, be sympathetic, accessible and knowledgeable about the candidate's area of interest;

- sufficiently senior to be in touch with the corporate structure, sharing the company's values and able to give the candidate access to resources and information;

- good teachers, able to advise and instruct without interfering, allowing candidates to explore and pursue ideas even though they may not be optimum pathways;

- good negotiators, willing and able to plan alongside their own management teams and academics'.[25]

Although a slightly dated report, (the CNAA no longer exists), it is an excellent description of the qualities necessary to make a good mentor and concurs with other texts on mentoring including Fisher.[26]

Clutterbuck[27] gives the following ten key core competencies:

1. self awareness (knowing oneself);
2. behavioural awareness (understanding others);
3. professional experience;
4. sense of proportion/humour;
5. communicating;
6. conceptualising;
7. commitment to own learning;
8. interest in developing others;
9. relationship management;
10. clarity of goals.

The above authors have all selected the same qualities that should be sought by the individual in the selection of a good mentor. Take time to seek out someone who can fulfil this role, even if it is not on a formal basis.

The mentee (protégé)

It is clear what is expected of the mentor in the mentoring process, but what should be expected of the mentee or protégé? Can anyone be a mentee or are there characteristics that can be identified in an individual that might indicate that they will benefit from the process?

To achieve some level of success the individual will benefit from mentoring if they have the following characteristics.

Personal ambition

If the individual is serious about their wish to develop, both personally and professionally then they will have some idea of where they want to be in a few years' time. This will drive them in following any development programme, so that they do not exclusively rely on the mentor, but use their guidance in developing their own skills through activities and actions.

Wish to be mentored

Anyone who is to benefit from mentoring must, obviously, want to be mentored. If the experience is unproductive then they may change their mind, but initially they must be willing to engage with the process and put their efforts into achieving the goals set by the mentor and themselves during the programme.

Context to their work

Mentors cannot be chosen at random; they must be someone who can offer support appropriate to the needs of the individual. Blandford[28] describes two roles in which mentoring will be effective. These are:

- vocational or career development;
- interpersonal or support for their current role.

The individual may have an interest in achieving professional status within their professional body, or developing their skills to improve their performance in their current role within the organisation. Whichever of these it is, the mentee must see that the mentor is able to offer support in one, or both, of these areas.

Building confidence

The mentee will often lack confidence in their skills. This is not surprising as they are developing their skills and will, at any moment in time, need to gain a skill or develop a skill to increase their competencies. In Chapter 2, using the LTSN portfolio for recording skills development in library and information science, we noted how skills are broken down into levels of increasing competency from basic to advanced. Confidence comes from the experience and knowledge that they gain when developing their skill-set. They will also benefit from the experience and knowledge of the mentor who will build up their confidence to enable them to move forward and develop both personally and professionally.

Willingness to learn

Again, an obvious statement, but if the individual has entered into a mentoring relationship without due consideration it will usually end in failure. The mentee must want to learn from the experience and knowledge that the mentor can offer. To do this they must willingly enter into a relationship that will enable them to learn from that experience.

Clear goals

The mentee must have a clear idea of what they wish to achieve from the process. They must have a clear idea of the skills they wish to develop or the career goals they want to achieve. The individual can then focus their attention on these, while benefiting from the support offered by the mentor.

Ability to analyse and reflect

Crucial to the development of any professional career is the ability both to analyse one's experience to determine exactly what has been learnt during the activity, and then to reflect on how this affects the way the individual will perform in the future, or the future direction they might take in the pursuit of their personal development. Reflection is a crucial skill to develop for the individual who is undertaking continuing professional development and other references to the importance of this skill can be found throughout the book.

Plan their career

Individuals who are actively trying to plan their career will benefit from mentoring for two reasons. First they will have someone who can offer an independent view on the path they wish to follow in their career. The mentor might offer impartial advice on some of their plans and guidance if they are unrealistic. Second they will be able to give the individual support in accessing career opportunities within their own organisation. Above all, the individual must have some idea of his or her own future direction so that maximum benefit can be gained from the process.

Need to develop personally

The individual must wish to develop personally. If the individual is planning their career then they will, almost certainly, be looking to develop the skills necessary for new and future roles. This need to develop personally should be combined with the use of a SWOT analysis, to determine strengths and weaknesses. The mentor will be able to use this analysis to guide the mentee in their development.

Need to develop professionally

Mentees will either be entering the profession for the first time or moving forward in their career with particular objectives in mind. Whichever is the case, they will be looking to develop their professional skills and standing to demonstrate their worth to their colleagues and the library and information community. This can be done in three ways:

- a shared organisational experience;
- through specialist help and expertise;
- through common interests.

The individual will develop more if the mentor is a member of the same organisation, largely because they will have a commonality of experience within the organisation. The mentor will consequently be able to talk to the mentee in terms that they will already understand.

If the mentor has developed a specialism in an area in which the individual is also interested in developing, then the individual will again benefit more from the relationship. The mentor will be able to help the mentee directly by imparting their own experience rather than referring them to another source.

Inevitably, if the mentor and mentee share common interests, whether professionally or otherwise, then both will benefit from the process. It enables a bond to develop which can lead to a greater sharing of experience and resources that will help to develop the individual.

The mentee will also benefit from unofficial mentoring in their everyday activities. They will be able to glean nuggets of useful information and advice from their peers, their line managers and other professionals with whom they may come into contact.

The mentoring process

The process is similar in some respects to the learning cycle previously discussed, but with some differences as more than one person is involved. Figure 5.1 shows the process as described by the Empathy Project[29] and reflects on the phases of the mentoring relationship that were described earlier in the chapter.

Figure 5.1   Phases of the mentoring process

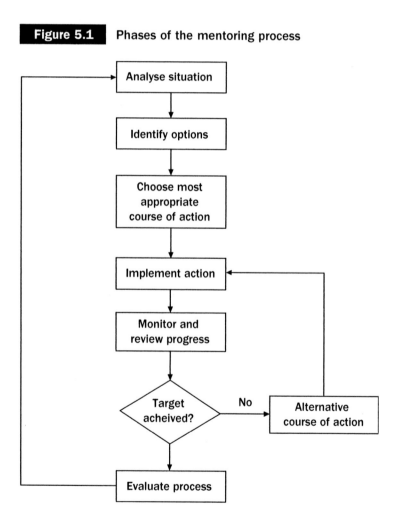

Beginning with an analysis of the situation, these activities provide a similar path to the learning cycle. Slight differences occur as the options are identified via a brainstorming session between mentor and mentee. Having identified and implemented the appropriate course of action, the mentee should review the process with the mentor, and determine whether the objectives have been met; after evaluation, the process should be started anew, or a different approach should be adopted.

Formal mentoring programmes

Having seen what is required from the participants in a successful mentoring relationship, what methods are available for the individual to take advantage of them? Formal mentoring programmes do exist, but unfortunately, they are uncommon in the library and information sector at present.

Some information professionals may discover that the organisation to which they belong operates a formal programme for mentoring, matching individuals to appropriate mentors for guidance. Even if the scheme does not focus on library and information work, if their employer has such a scheme, then the individual can still take advantage of the process.

It is highly likely that programmes of this nature will only be found in larger corporate structures, for example, Fisher quotes The Miami-Dade Community College, a large multi-campus community college in the USA,[30] while Conway quotes the likes of BT in the UK (in the telecommunications sector) and ABB in Sweden (in the automation and power technologies industry).[31] Both Yale University Library[32] and the University of Maryland University Libraries[33] both operate mentoring schemes. These allow individuals to volunteer for the process and to choose their mentoring partner. No member of staff is excluded from the process and the schemes specifically state that their goals are to support personal and professional development.

The programme will include the following personnel:

- mentor;
- mentee;
- line manager;
- coordinator.

The first two have been previously discussed in this chapter. The line manager is also crucial to the mentoring programme, as they are possibly in the best position to identify when a mentor might be able to help an individual with their personal development. Any advice or assistance that the mentor has given to the individual cannot be effectively actioned without the support of the line manager. The line manager is able to action training for their staff and so meet their training needs. This may also feed into staff development, appraisal programmes or other organisational programmes that exist to develop the workforce. It is essential that the line manager is involved as they will ensure the development of the individual, clarify people's roles and ensure no confusion arises between those involved.

The coordinator of the mentoring programme may be in sole charge (if it is a large programme) or they may be the staff development manager or equivalent. Their role may well include matching mentors and mentees, as well as being responsible for conveying the operation of the programme to all those involved. During the process they will help to enable any requests for training, where they lie outside the immediate power of the line manager. They will also, most importantly, provide training for mentors, so that the maximum benefit will be gained from the process for all those involved.

There is one further necessity for a mentoring programme: the need for senior management support. No scheme will succeed unless it has the backing of senior members of the organisation and that those same backers are seen to be supportive of the programme.

Benefits of mentoring

The process of mentoring brings benefits to all those involved. According to the National Library Board of Singapore[34] they include, for the mentee:

- advice on career planning, personal and professional development;
- acquisition of new skills;
- understanding about career development;
- widening of networking circle;
- support in managing change and difficulties;
- boost to self-esteem;
- encouragement to take up new projects and responsibilities;
- insight into organisational policies;
- enhanced management skills;
- reduced professional isolation.

New entrants to the profession, who have come directly from university, will gain a better induction into their organisation if they have been allocated a mentor. This is emphasised by the other benefits they would receive, which would also benefit other new employees, for example, that that mentors will help introduce them to the structure of the organisation and will provide career advancement within the organisation through their advice.

This advice can also help them to begin their managerial career through the tutelage of the mentor. With the right support the mentor will build up the confidence of the individual and help to develop their skills and potential.

The mentor will also gain benefits from the process, as will the line manager. The National Library Board[35] gives the benefits for the mentor as:

- personal satisfaction;
- development of professional skills, such as counselling;
- incentive to keep abreast of professional developments;
- exposure to new ideas and different perspectives of the profession;
- widening of professional network;
- career enhancement;
- giving something back to the profession.

By developing another professional, the mentor will gain an increased sense of job satisfaction and will also gain increased recognition from their peers once they see the outcome of their efforts. This can include the individual's own line manager who might benefit from the mentee being able to access a second opinion if they are having difficulties understanding some aspect of their work. The line manager may also benefit from the mentee being able to develop relationships with their colleagues and their line manager having gone through the process of developing a relationship with their mentor.

Both the organisation and the profession will benefit from the mentoring process. The National Library Board[36] emphasises the benefits for the organisation as:

- increased productivity;
- improvement in managers skills;
- more flexible organisation;
- staff empowerment;
- increased commitment from new and experienced staff;
- increased understanding of organisations goals;
- lower staff turnover;
- less staff burnout;
- enhanced learning culture;
- leadership and successor planning.

For the profession they state that the benefits are:

- promotion of professional development;
- enhanced professionalism within the profession;
- understanding of wider professional issues and trends;
- promotion of professional vision;
- development of professional networking and support mechanisms;
- support for disadvantaged groups in the profession.

The process of mentoring provides benefits for all of the personnel involved, but most importantly will benefit both the organisation they work for and the profession itself.

No programme?

Even if one is not lucky enough to have a formal mentoring programme it is still possible to gain the benefit of mentoring on an informal basis. As already stated they will be able to get support and advice from their peers, their line managers and other professionals with whom they may come into contact. This can occur during any of the networking activities mentioned at the beginning of this chapter.

Although not technically termed mentoring schemes, there are other ways of obtaining advice from experienced library and information professionals aside from the *ad hoc* methods mentioned at the beginning of the chapter. Individuals may benefit from another's experience if they take part in staff appraisals, development reviews or any other supervisory process. An example of a useful scheme would be the Chartership scheme run by CILIP[37] in the UK. Those candidates who are following an approved scheme that has been ratified by the Chartership Board at CILIP will have a supervisor for their programme. This supervisor will act as a sounding board for their professional development and help to shepherd them in undertaking activities to enhance their professional experience. This might include suggesting events for them to attend, ensuring that they have covered all the relevant aspects of their programme or arranging for them to meet other library and information professionals in different organisations and sectors. Additionally, the supervisor will be able to offer advice from their own experience to guide the candidate in creating their own professional development portfolio to present to the professional body in order to achieve their Chartership and consequent post-nominals. Should the opportunity arise to partake in a scheme of this nature then the individual should give it serious consideration as it can deliver considerable benefits.

Financial implications

Many of the activities that have been described in this chapter have financial implications for the individual and this can have an untoward effect on one's ability to take advantage of the training opportunity. Courses are often too expensive for the individual to fund from their own resources. It is, therefore, important that the individual seeks funding from other sources. There are a number of possibilities, including:

- the employer;
- event organisers;
- professional associations and groups;
- educational establishments.

Employers

The individual will often first try to obtain funding for attendance at a training event from their employer. Many employers will pay for attendance at an event as long as it is work-related. One should not always assume that this is true in all cases – the employer may have committed their training budget to the organisation of internal training courses; the budget may be of a limited size so that only a handful of staff are able to attend external events; the employer may not see the benefits of training library and information staff.

In the first instance, individuals should take advantage of the internal training courses, whether related to health and safety or other aspects of their working environment. In the second, it will be important to make a good case to your employer as to why you should be able to attend the event: look at what the event promises and relate that directly to your role within the organisation, stating the benefits that will be brought about by your attendance at the course. For example, are you prepared to offer cascade training on your return to the workplace for others? Will you be able to provide a new dimension to the service that was not previously available? Can you provide improvements to an existing service if you attend? Be prepared to argue your case and be clear why you wish to go. Finally, if your employer does not see the benefit of training the library and information staff, you must again argue the benefits of training and professional development. They will have other staff requiring professional development, whether in the legal, medical, engineering or other professions and could be made to realise the importance of development of their library and information staff; just be clear about the benefits of an individual's attendance at an event to themselves and the organisation.

Event organisers

Some events, especially conferences, make subsidised places available for attendees, especially if they are a first time attendee or have recently joined the profession. The International Federation of Library Associations and Institutions, for example, provide places for attendees from poorer countries so that they can benefit from the expertise at the IFLA conference and to network with others, thus enabling their own professional development. Many large conferences offer discounts to students so that they may attend professional conferences during their period of study. This is of huge benefit to both their study and their future professional development as it provides an indication of the benefits of professional development while the individual is aspiring to become a fully functioning member of the library and information community.

Professional associations

It is not always obvious, but most professional associations provide bursaries for those in the profession to attend relevant events. CILIP in the UK provides funding for new attendees to IFLA's conference and also gives discounts to individuals who are registered to become chartered members.

Sections or groups within associations, and other professional groups, also offer discounts to their events and subsidised places at their conferences. The Career Development Group (CDG)[38] offers a free place at their conference to anyone who is new to the profession. It would be impossible to note here all of the professional groups and the opportunities that they offer, but individuals should look at the opportunities afforded to them at both a national, regional and local level.

Educational establishments

Individuals should contact library schools to see if any of their courses offer funding. Some courses, such as Masters degrees, are sometimes afforded funding by educational funding bodies in the country concerned. In the UK the Arts and Humanities Research Board (AHRB) offers funding for some Masters courses in library and information science as well as for those applying for PhD funding within the discipline. Different funding mechanisms are to be found in each country and individuals will have to investigate availability in their own country and this is best achieved by contacting the library schools or the relevant professional association.

Summary

There are many sources of support for the individual intent on following a course of continuing professional development. Careful consideration should be given to the methods that one would like to use, while also keeping a watching brief for any unexpected opportunities that might come to pass.

Networking is one of the strongest methods to ensure that the individual develops in a professional manner and maintains strong links with the professional community. Personal contacts and colleagues are important methods for obtaining guidance on professional issues that affect both their immediate work environment and their professional development. Contacts can be cultivated at training events and courses to the benefit of the individual. Training events are the perfect time to speak to other professionals who work in similar or even different environments and share good practice. Strong bonds can develop between individuals, leading to the formation of small communities that support each other. These can become discussion groups via online forums at a later stage thus allowing geographically disparate groups to continue to share and develop professionally. The individual can also access both weblogs and newsfeeds to keep abreast of the latest developments in areas of specific interest.

The process of mentoring traditionally cultivates a relationship between a master and apprentice and has been productive over time. The experienced master would train and develop the skills of the apprentice so that the skills would be carried forward to future generations. Mentoring has changed considerably over the years, but the concept remains the same at its core: skills and knowledge are passed on from one experienced individual to someone who is less experienced. The benefits of the process are many and varied, but ostensibly they are that the individual:

- receives advice about aspects of career planning;
- receives professional development support;
- acquires new skills;
- gains greater understanding of their career development;
- widens their own network of contacts;
- receives support in managing change;
- boosts their self-confidence.

New projects and responsibilities that the individual might undertake will be encouraged and supported, while through regular contact with their mentor, they will gain an insight into organisational policies and grasp an insight into managerial skills.

There are further benefits of the mentoring process to both the organisation and the profession. If an individual is actively improving themselves and their service, the employer benefits from an improved service, while the profession gains a more adept and involved individual.

Financial assistance can be of paramount importance to some individuals, but if sought, support in this area can be obtained from employers, educational bodies and professional organisations.

Support can be found in many guises, but it will not seek out the individual. Even the best advertised offers of support need to be actively sought and then acted upon by the individual. Continuing professional develop does not just happen to individuals, it needs to be sought and undertaken by the individual themselves, if it is, then the benefits for all are easily seen.

Notes

1. British Computer Society. *BCS European Computer Driving Licence: http://www.ecdl.co.uk/* (visited 25 June 2004).
2. 7 Seconds Resources Inc. *TechTutorials: Free Computer Reference: http://www.techtutorials.com/* (visited 25 June 2004).
3. Blackboard Inc. *Blackboard Worldwide: http://www .blackboard.com/* (visited 25 June 2004).
4. WebCT Inc. *WebCT: Learning without Limits: http://www .webct.com/* (visited 25 June 2004).
5. Eduserv. *Eduserv Athens for Education: http://www.athens .ac.uk/* (visited 25 June 2004).
6. The Open University. *The Open University: http://www.open .ac.uk/* (visited 25 June 2004).
7. T. Anderson and H. Kanuka (1997) On-line Forums: New Platforms for Professional Development and Group Collaboration. *Journal of Computer-mediated Communication,* 3: *http://www.ascusc.org/jcmc/vol3/issue3/anderson.html* (visited 17 September 2004).
8. R. Bernier and J.P. Bowen (2004) Web-based Discussion Groups at Stake: the Profile of Museum Professionals Online. *Program: Electronic Library and Information Systems,* 38: 120–137.
9. Aycan Gulez. *WowBB: Wow Bulletin Board: http://www .wowbb.com/* (visited 12 July 2004).
10. L-soft. *Email Marketing, Email List and Mail Server Software – L-Soft: http://www.lsoft.com/* (visited 25 June 2004).
11. Great Circle Associates Inc. *Majordomo: http://www .greatcircle.com/majordomo/* (visited 25 June 2004).
12. American Library Association. *List of ALA Discussion Groups: http://www.ala.org/ala/ourassociation/discussiongroups/ listaladiscussion.htm* (visited 12 July 2004).

13. Google. *Google Groups: http://groups.google.com/* (visited 25 June 2004).
14. P. Pedley (2004) Have You Thought of Blogging? *Library and Information Update*, 3: 32–33.
15. Google. *Blogger: http://www.blogger.com/* (visited 25 June 2004).
16. P. Scott. *Library Weblogs from around the World: http://www.libdex.com/weblogs.html* (visited 25 June 2004).
17. I. Winship (2004) Weblogs and RSS in Information Work. *Library and Information Update*, 3: 30–31.
18. D. Levinson (1978) *The Season's of a Man's Life.* New York: Alfred Knopf.
19. D. Clutterbuck (2001) *Everyone Needs a Mentor: Fostering Talent at Work.* 3rd edn. London: Chartered Institute of Personnel and Development: p. 3.
20. E. Parsloe (1992) *Coaching, Mentoring and Assessing: a Practical Guide to Developing Competence.* London: Kogan Page.
21. D. Clutterbuck, *op cit.* pp. 16–18.
22. Ibid., pp. 19–21.
23. University of Hull, Business School. *The Empathy Project E-mentoring Guidelines: http://www.hull.ac.uk/hubs/empathy/documents/Mentoring%20Guidance%20for%203rd%20Year%20HUBS%20Students.doc* (visited 20 April 2004).
24. E. Parsloe (1995) *The Manager as Coach and Mentor.* London: Institute of Personnel and Development; pp. 25–26.
25. Ibid.
26. B. Fisher (1994) *Mentoring.* London: Library Association Publishing: pp. 4–10.
27. D. Clutterbuck (2000) Ten Core Mentor Competencies. *Organisations and People*, 7(2): 29–34.
28. S. Blandford (2000) *Managing Professional Development in Schools.* London: Routledge; p. 180.
29. University of Hull, Business School *op cit.*
30. B. Fisher, *op cit.* p. 27.
31. C. Conway (1998) *Strategies for Mentoring: a Blueprint for Successful Organisational Development.* Chichester: John Wiley; pp. 79–93.

32. Yale University Library. *SCOPA Mentoring Program for the Yale University Library:* http://www.library.yale.edu/scopa/mentoring/mentoring.html (visited 17 September 2004).

33. University Libraries, University of Maryland. *Mentoring Program:* http://www.lib.umd.edu/ASD/LPO/mentoring/index.html (visited 6 July 2004).

34. The National Library Board. *Mentoring: Information Services Topical Brief:* http://www.consal.org.sg/webupload/resource/brief/attachments/%7B6FFF607C-3A70-4D43-884E-B10A4FE70B45%7D.pdf (visited 17 September 2004).

35. Ibid.

36. Ibid.

37. Chartered Institute of Library and Information Professionals. *Chartered Membership:* http://www.cilip.org.uk/qualifications/chartering.html (visited 1 June 2004).

38. Career Development Group. *Career Development Group: Homepage:* http://www.careerdevelopmentgroup.org.uk/index.htm (visited 25 June 2004).

6

Continuing career development?

Continuing professional development is essential for the library and information worker to ensure that their skills and competencies remain current. This will maintain the reputation of the professional and the service that they are providing to users. Most information professionals will see this as their reason for continually renewing and developing their skill-set. However, the individual should not see this as their only reason for building upon previous development, it is entirely valid to use the process as a vehicle for progressing one's career.

The library and information sector is not the same now as it was ten years ago and will be different again in another ten years. Metadata and knowledge management are current expressions used by many in the library and information sector, but still express aspects of information work and require the skills of capturing, organising and maintaining that are the bedrock of the information professional's skills. Modern developments, including the use of new tools to achieve these, mean that the individual must adapt to be able to maintain their skills, protect their employability and their career enhancement.

Progressing one's career should not be thought of as 'climbing up the ladder' within the organisation. The individual should develop their skills not only to move into management but to enable them to cope with the vagaries of the job market and future employment. Whereas in the past, individuals have been able to remain in the same post for many years, it is now much more likely that change will occur equally within the organisation or in the wider library and information sector. The development of one's skills is essential because many organisations now undertake restructuring exercises to maximise cost benefits and staff may find themselves undertaking a new role, or at worst, looking for a new position. In any event, having a diverse and developed skill-set will prepare the individual for many eventualities.

Many of the methods discussed in previous chapters should also be used to help plan one's career development. Some will be mentioned again to remind ourselves of their importance and some will be approached in a different manner to guide the individual towards the goal of career progression.

Pantry and Griffiths in *Your Essential Guide to Career Success*[1] emphasise the need for continuing professional development. They state that a library service must have 'appropriately trained staff' to be effective and that to ensure that this is maintained a 'supply of new information and library professionals with these skills is required'. Finally, their most important point, as previously emphasised, is that 'the existing workforce must upgrade their skills to meet these new and constant challenges'.

Many writers have written about career development including Layzell Ward,[2] Shontz[3] and Townsend Kane.[4] The material covered in their publications and others cannot hope to be covered here, therefore, the intention is to relate areas where continuing professional development intersects with the development of the individual's career in the library and information sector or any of the many allied sectors, such as publishing, computing and other non-traditional roles.

Skills assessment

Previous chapters have reviewed the acquisition of new skills and those processes that can be used to record and track their development. Emphasis should also be placed on the individual's career development. Some individuals may prefer to plan ahead for a particular role, possibly even at a particular level. Others are less proactive and wish to take advantage of opportunities as they arise.

Evans, Layzell Ward and Rugaas[5] state that the following should be considered when making a personal assessment of one's skills to plan for any future career:

- level of qualifications;
- short courses attended;
- study currently being undertaken;
- professional activities;
- committee work within the organisation;
- work experience;
- preferred career direction;
- preferred sector;
- preferred specialisation;
- areas currently not under consideration by the individual;
- personal strengths;
- personal weaknesses;
- commitment to librarianship and information work in the long term;
- external factors that are personally important and may restrict professional growth.

In many ways this is another checklist that the individual can complete and use to help them maintain their original plan towards a specific career goal, or more importantly, it can be used in conjunction with a professional development portfolio. Using it in conjunction with, or as part of, a portfolio can enable the individual both to plan their career and adapt their plans at appropriate moments in their career. It is not unknown to find trained librarians moving into other sectors ranging from computing, to teaching and even insurance and legal work. This is because the skills obtained by library and information workers cover an extremely wide area making them both highly employable and adaptable. A post as a librarian may begin as the long-term career goal for many, but information work pervades every other sector in many different guises and the individual should be mindful of this fact as they progress along their chosen path. Sellen, in *What Else You Can Do with a Library Degree*,[6] provides a much more comprehensive idea of the opportunities available to those trained in library and information work than can be included here, but the options are many and varied. Whatever the individual decides to do with their degree, there should be no less emphasis on professional development and planning using a portfolio.

Evans, Layzell Ward and Rugaas argue that the individual should perform a regular self-assessment as it will assist in career development. Many of the points that they raise in the list above have been indicated in previous chapters as necessary for inclusion in a portfolio for professional development. Strengths and weaknesses, study undertaken, professional activities and courses attended should all be included in a portfolio as a matter of course. Those items that would not necessarily be included are those that could be argued to be of a more personal nature, such as external factors that may affect one's career path. In truth, however, these may have more of an impact than any qualification or training undertaken on the future direction of the individual's career. Marriage, children, health or any other change in circumstances may change the direction in which one's career is heading or even put it on hold. Whatever the case, it would be an informed professional who at least maintains a watching brief on those factors that can affect their career or, even better, keeps a written record of their plans so that they can adapt as circumstances dictate in the future.

Career planning

Career planning is essential if one is to remain on track for one's original career goal. This does not mean that the individual should not change and adapt to take advantage of new opportunities, but planning, like professional development, should be a continuous process. The continuously evolving library and information environment will present more and more opportunities for the committed professional; however, it also means that it is harder, and therefore essential, to plan and keep a record of that plan.

It is rare to find oneself in a post that will last for most of one's employed lifetime. There are very few posts in the sector that will enable this, and more importantly, organisational and sectoral changes and upheavals make this an even more remote possibility. Some individuals may find that they have worked their way 'up the ladder' in larger organisations, or at least stayed in the same sector; however, it is becoming increasingly common to find that individuals make frequent job changes to progress their careers. This is sometimes known as a 'portfolio career' and is more prevalent in some sectors, such as financial services, than others. What is clear is that following a portfolio career requires that the individual spends more time reviewing their skills and planning their career.

When reviewing one's career development, adopting a method that will aid planning could be useful. Many will probably do this unconsciously, whether through perusing the job pages in the relevant professional or national press or by some other self-determined method. Pantry and Griffiths have suggested a model which they have named the 'AEIOU model'.[7]

The AEIOU model suggests the following steps in assessing the risks at any point in an individual's career:

1. assess;

2. evaluate;

3. improve;

4. observe;

5. update.

The first step requires assessing the hazards of one's current job. Is it the right kind of work, in the wrong part of the country, or does it present any other barriers according to future career plans? Pantry and Griffiths suggest approaching the employer or line manager to ask about one's own prospects and skills. This is perfectly acceptable, but why not approach a mentor if one is lucky enough to have one, or even other colleagues within the organisation? They may provide valid feedback to the individual. The individual must also list the positives as well, as it may not be an appropriate time at which to move into another phase of one's career. However, it is important to note down those areas that the individual is working towards and the progress being made towards them.

The second step is to document the positives and negatives and evaluate whether the best option is to stay with one's current employer and follow opportunities available within the organisation or to invest one's energies towards the prospects of a new beginning elsewhere.

Improving one's current position through the introduction of some appropriate training or by undertaking some new activities, such as managing a project, may help the individual to overcome some of the minuses currently prohibiting their career development.

Consistently observing one's progress towards the positives and negatives that were discovered and noted down in the first stage will provide the individual with a reminder of where they are going and what they need to undertake to get there. It will also enable them to see if they have veered too far from their original objectives and whether the original plan is still valid.

Lastly, the individual must update the original assessment. This should be carried out at least on a yearly basis so that the individual can feed their needs into any review in the workplace and also factor in any major changes that affect their career direction.

This may seem a trifle over-zealous but it is carried out by most people on a frequent basis anyway; what many will not do, however, is actually commit the process to paper. Everyone wonders whether they have enough annual leave, reasonable pay for what they do, prospects for training and development and will consider if they are happy in their current position or not. Formalising this process will do most individuals no harm at all and more often will do some good.

Setting career goals

Traditional patterns of employment would have meant that the individual might spend their whole career working their way up through a single organisation. Today career patterns are much more flexible and one may change employer and even sector on a frequent basis. However, the factors that lead to the successful progression in one's career are consistent. The individual must always pay close attention to their:

- qualifications;
- experience;
- attitude; and
- aptitude.

To some these may seem obvious, but when prospective employers are looking at CVs, application forms and even interviewing candidates they will be looking for these attributes. They will be assessing whether the individual's qualifications match those that are required in the person specification for a post, and that same individual must also match the required levels of experience for the specification. Both attitude and aptitude will be judged on one's application and interview with the employer. Additionally, many jobs that involve information professionals also require that the individual make a formal presentation to a specified group as well as an interview. This tests the individual's skills and demonstrates their attitude and aptitude to the prospective employer. Paying attention to the above four bullet points will help the individual in preparing themselves for any future attempts at changing or furthering their career directions.

Setting career goals will provide a standard against which the individual can measure their current level of skills. Looking at the factors above and then noting the level one believes they are currently at, gives the individual a clear checklist of skills they should attain and the activities they need to undertake to achieve this level.

Career goals will change throughout one's personal and professional life. Committing them to paper will remind the individual to check that any training and skills acquisition they undertake is moving them towards those goals. It will enable them to judge whether other opportunities that arise, such as a new job, will also fit the plan the individual has prepared.

Throughout career progression, the skills one will use will change, depending on the job in which the individual finds themselves.

Management skills

As their career develops, the individual acquires new skills, including managerial skills; if they are not acquiring them then they need to obtain them to progress in their career. Many generic skills are important for managing staff and these should be developed whenever the opportunity arises, not when one has achieved a management position. Communication skills, for example, are one such area and are essential for anyone wishing to make the most of managerial opportunities. Communicating effectively with staff is one of the most important facets of good management. Adopting good practice in these areas will benefit the individual. Another important area is that of supervisory skills and the information professional should seize any opportunity that allows supervising staff, whether it comes in the form of a 'one-off' project or through a specific activity. Gaining some grounding in supervision of staff will give the individual a start in how to deal with staff in different situations. In many ways, experience is paramount as the different permutations of how staff will act in any given situation are endless.

One method that individuals might use to improve their skills is through mentoring. This has already been covered in previous chapters but it is worth consolidating due to the benefits that it can provide. One should consider both approaching a senior information professional who might provide some guidance in this area and also consider being a mentor to somebody else in the profession. The experience of providing guidance on personal and professional development for somebody else often acts as a catalyst for one's own thoughts on personal development.

In the past, many library and information professionals may have thought that their training was at an end after completing their professional qualifications in library and information science. If this ever was the case, it certainly is no longer. Professionals do not have to gain management skills 'on the job' although this is still perfectly valid, and should be used in conjunction with other methods. This includes the ubiquitous MBA which has become more important to information professionals if they wish to develop their career and attain management positions. With the constantly changing boundaries in the information profession it is increasingly likely that library and information professionals will find themselves competing against non-information professionals for managerial positions.

New skills?

Attaining management skills should not be seen as the only way to develop one's career. Library and information professionals can develop their teaching or training skills to follow alternative routes that will bring both personal and financial rewards equal to those offered by some management positions. Equally, more technical skills could be developed, especially those required in library systems work, such as web-based skills, which will provide those same rewards.

Other new skills may be required for future information professionals. Web-based skills are the most obvious growth area for information professionals, both in the handling of metadata for online resources and information, and in the design and creation of delivery through databases and websites. Lavoie and O'Neill[8] carried out research to determine how international the World Wide Web truly was. They discovered that between June 1998 and June 1999 there was a 28% increase in the number of countries with public websites. Further to this they found that there was a 21% increase in the number of languages that were used on these sites. This shows that there may be a need for library and information professionals, who have a command of other languages and are proficient in the use of the Internet. This will ensure full searching of all available information on the Internet for some employers.

Library and information professionals will always be required and their importance to both the commercial and public sectors should not be underestimated. However, they often are underestimated, and it is likely that there will be a decrease in full-time permanent posts in the information profession. In this scenario it may be found that information professionals are 'called in' on a consultancy basis to provide solutions to information-related problems within organisations. This in turn may lead to a need for more consultancy skills in the profession.

Finally, it should be remembered that librarians and information professionals have an extremely wide base of skills, many of these generic. This puts individuals in a strong position to develop their career in many and varied directions should they choose to do so.

Career advice and direction

Earlier in this chapter it was stated that this book does not try to reproduce those sources already available for career development. Consequently interviewing, preparing CVs and application forms, researching the job market and alternative career paths are not considered here in any depth. Readers should review the sources highlighted in the following section, but also seek out their own resources which may be equally valuable.

One important point to note, however, is to promote the importance of CVs to the library and information professional. Much has been made of the importance of portfolios in previous chapters, but one of the most important building blocks in a portfolio is the CV. For the purpose of a job application the CV provides the prospective employer with a brief résumé of your career, experience and skills acquired to date. This is made much easier for the individual if their portfolio contains all the relevant information which can be condensed into the smaller CV. The CV, if constantly maintained, should also act as a guide to the portfolio, reflecting the individual's current level of skills and development. Further information should be sought on what makes a good CV, and on the type of format that best suits each individual, from the following and other sources.

Career development websites

Notable text resources have already been quoted at the beginning of this chapter and are located in the notes section at the end of this chapter. Here the discussion revolves around those websites that can provide some help and/or guidance for the individual. Those websites of note, dedicated to career development for librarians and information professionals, are online companions to text resources on career development. Liscareer.com[9] is headed 'The Library and Information Science Professional's Career Development Center' and provides links to resources, both print and online, and also some practical advice. The site was created as a companion to *Jump Start Your Career in Library and Information Science* by Priscilla Shontz[10] and will also act as a companion to *The Librarian's Career Guidebook*[11] by the same author.

The Information Professional's Guide to Career Development Online[12] is the companion website to the publication of the same name.[13] This has been created by the authors Sarah L. Nesbeitt and Rachel Singer Gordon. This provides useful links to all URLs mentioned in their text publication and some other useful links to seminars and weblogs. It should be clearly noted, however, that despite their usefulness they are maintained by authors with strong links to their own publications and consequently these sites are primarily for this purpose. This does not diminish their usefulness, but the individual should also look elsewhere for resources on career development.

Professional

One of the best methods of support for career development is through the individual's own professional association. They can provide support in many different ways from mentoring to publications and websites. Many of these support mechanisms have already been covered in previous chapters, so reference here will only be made to online resources available so that readers can then access and make their own judgments about them.

The American Library Association (ALA)[14] provides links to websites on career development on a variety of library and information careers, from those in law to library schools. They also provide a comprehensive set of links to general careers websites that provide useful information if the correct search terms are used to access information on the site. Text resources are not omitted and a good list of career guidance publications is located on the site.

The Special Libraries Association (SLA) has developed an extremely useful resource for the sector which covers many areas, including careers. The Librarian's Resource Centre (LRC)[15] has a searchable database on a variety of resources for librarians, covering not just careers, but also other topics that individuals can use in their professional development, ranging from weblogs, through to education to management.

The Chartered Institute for Library and Information Professionals[16] in the UK provides a website for its members that gives access to the latest job vacancies as well as useful information on job hunting, salaries and professional practice. Although not a vast resource it has been growing steadily over time and looks set to grow further with the advent of validation for professional practice within the UK.

Finally, the Australian Library and Information Association (ALIA) deserves a mention due to the online support it provides to its members. ALIA has introduced validation for its members to help raise the profession's profile among employers and to provide evidence that the skills of librarians are current and valid. To this end ALIA has developed recording mechanisms for the development of portfolios, as described in earlier chapters, and has also provided a career development kit to support members. The career development kit gives the individual a framework for their continuing professional development and consequently their career development. The kit aims to help individuals:

- analyse professional development needs;
- set objectives to meet these needs;
- gain input from others, such as mentors and line managers;
- build a repository for this knowledge;
- determine priorities for the future.[17]

It provides guidance and examples on how to undertake the process and methods of recording one's progress.

Professional associations can provide good quality support for the individual should they choose to use it. The most important point that should be made at this point, which has been made by ALIA in their career development kit is that continuing professional development is virtually synonymous with career development. A library and information professional who is constantly developing and updating their skill-set will find that their career develops, even if the direction is unexpected.

Summary

It is evident that the library and information professional of today needs to continually develop their skills and competencies to ensure that they remain competitive in the job market. The continuously changing nature of the library and information sector with the development of new specialities, such as the creation of web-based resources and services, provides many more opportunities for information professionals, but it also presents many challenges and the need for continuous professional development.

To ensure the individual is ready to adapt to any future change of circumstances they should make certain that their skill-set is as current as possible. This requires that the individual assesses their skills at regular intervals with a view to possible future career directions. Reviewing one's strengths and weaknesses, reviewing training undertaken and assessing future areas of work are all required if the individual is to adequately assess their career development. At this point they can make an informed choice about their future career direction and even determine whether it still remains in the library and information sector.

Information professionals should adopt some form of career planning from an early stage, recording their goals so that at any given moment they can reflect on their progress and decide whether they should make any changes to their original objectives or whether they need to strengthen their portfolio through the addition of more skills and training to meet those original goals. Setting career goals is important; if this is to be successful then attention should be paid to one's qualifications, experience, attitude and aptitudes. Prospective employers will look for all of these qualities and judge the individual's ability for any given post, so it is important that the individual also assesses themselves in the same way.

As their career develops, many library and information professionals will ascend to the ranks of management and will need to acquire these skills either before or after they find themselves in a management post. The individual must, therefore, look for the opportunity to develop these skills, possibly through projects or secondments, to prepare themselves for the future. Equally, it is entirely valid for the individual to grasp any opportunity to develop their career in any chosen direction, even if this ignores managerial skills and allows them to develop skills in more specialist areas.

There are many sources of help that the individual can approach from online resources to professional associations.

Some suggestions have been made here but it is more important that the individual search for the resources that best suit them and plan their career development accordingly. In the final analysis it is the individual who is responsible for their continuing professional development and consequently their career development.

Notes

1. S. Pantry and P. Griffiths (2003) *Your Essential Guide to Career Success*. 2nd edn. London: Facet Publishing; pp. 12–16.
2. P. Layzell Ward (ed) (1980) *The Professional Development of the Librarian and Information Worker*. London: Aslib.
3. P. Shontz (2002) *Jump Start Your Career in Library and Information Science*. Lanham, MD: Scarecrow Press.
4. L. Townsend Kane (2003) *Straight from the Stacks: A First-Hand Guide to Careers in Library and Information Science*. Chicago, IL: American Library Association (ALA).
5. G.E. Evans, P. Layzell Ward and B. Rugaas. *Career Development* (Chapter 20): *http://www.neal-schuman.com/career.htm* (visited 1 July 2004).
6. B.-C. Sellen (ed.) (1997) *What Else You Can Do With a Library Degree: Career Options for the 90's and Beyond*. New York: Neal-Schuman.
7. S. Pantry and P. Griffiths, *op. cit.*, pp. 20–21.
8. B.F. Lavoie and E.T. O'Neill. *How 'World Wide' Is the Web? Trends in the Internationalization of Web Sites: http://digitalarchive.oclc.org/da/ViewObject.jsp?objid=0000003496* (visited 5 October 2004).
9. P. Shontz. *Liscareer.com: The Librarian & Information Professional's Career Development Center: http://www.liscareer.com/* (visited 1 July 2004).
10. Ibid.
11. P. Shontz (2004) *The Librarian's Career Guidebook*. Lanham, MD: Scarecrow Press.

12. S.L. Nesbeitt, and R. Singer Gordon. *The Information Professional's Guide to Career Development Online: http://www.lisjobs.com/careerdev/index.htm* (visited 20 August 2004).

13. S.L. Nesbeitt, and R. Singer Gordon (2004) *The Information Professional's Guide to Career Development Online.* Medford, NJ: Information Today.

14. American Library Association. *Careers in Libraries: http://www.ala.org/ala/hrdr/careersinlibraries/careerslibraries.htm* (visited 17 September 2004).

15. Special Libraries Association. *Librarian's Resource Centre* (homepage and site map): *http://www.sla.org/chapter/ctor/toolbox/resource/cover.htm* (visited 20 August 2004).

16. Chartered Institute for Library and Information Professionals. *LIS jobnet – Information for Jobseekers/Career Entrants: http://www.lisjobnet.org.uk/jobseek/libindex.html* (visited 1 July 2004).

17. Australian Library and Information Association. *The ALIA Career Development Kit* (September 2003): *http://www.alia.org.au/education/cpd/career.kit.html* (visited 17 September 2004).

7

Summary

Continuing professional development is a lifelong commitment to one's own improvement. It is a process that involves ritual self assessment to ensure that the individual's development does not stagnate and adapts to the needs of the profession, the employer and the individual themselves. To ensure that stagnation does not occur, the preceding chapters have provided a framework and helpful advice so that the individual can support their own development. Although professionals will not utilise all of these techniques they can take and adapt those best suited to their circumstances.

Planning

The key to professional development is planning. The book has referred throughout to checklists that enable the individual to analyse their skills, check their progress and how to find support. All of these require the individual to continuously self assess, reflect and look ahead. As long as this is kept in mind then one can develop skills in a professional manner at any given point in one's career.

The development cycle

The process of developing skills is similar to that of learning. Kolb[1] describes the 'learning cycle' as having four stages which are cyclical in nature and should all take place to be fully effective.

The cycle has been used by other writers, as previously discussed, to express the process in the following stages:

- planning;
- doing;
- recording;
- reviewing;
- evaluating.

The first looks at how to achieve change, followed by learning by experience and then providing evidence of the experience. It finishes with the individual's reflection on the experience and judgments on their own development and further work they need to carry out.

The reflective practitioner

Three forms of reflection have been described.

'Reflection on action',[2] whereby the individual undertakes an activity and then reviews how well it went, whether they achieved what they wanted and why.

'Reflection in action',[3] which is at the heart of professional practice along with professional knowledge. The practitioner will reflect on their activities and adjust what they do on a daily basis. This activity is difficult to analyse and even harder to provide evidence for.

'Reflection for action'[4] is carried out by the individual so they can plan for future development.

These three kinds of reflection will all be performed by the individual during the creation of a portfolio and are the key to creating a successful portfolio.

Honey and Mumford[5] quote four learning styles that can be adopted by individuals, these being:

- activist;
- reflector;
- theorist;
- pragmatist.

Individuals will exhibit tendencies of one or more of these styles, but only some will be natural reflectors. However, there are ways in which individuals can improve their reflective abilities.

Improving reflection

The individual can improve their ability to reflect through these methods:

- observe the behaviour of others, both verbal and non-verbal;
- keep a regular record of events and reflect on activities to see if any conclusions can be drawn from these;
- review meetings or events and see if any lessons can be learnt from them;
- carry out some research that requires gathering data;
- write something that needs to be professionally presented, e.g. a report or paper;
- produce arguments for and against a particular course of action.

Skills, strengths and weaknesses

Professionals, in any field of expertise, should be aware of their strengths and weaknesses. These can be separated into:

- skills currently possessed;
- those to be acquired.

To ensure that skills are acquired to the appropriate level individuals should follow an appropriate path of continuing professional development that analyses those skills they already have, including their strengths and weaknesses, and builds upon these to create an improved set of skills to support their chosen career.

Strengths and weaknesses are fundamental to any individual's continuing professional development. They need to be examined and then listed both honestly and openly. Commonly, strengths and weaknesses should be investigated in a SWOT analysis as described by Boydell and Leary:[6]

- strengths;
- weaknesses;
- opportunities;
- threats.

Performing a SWOT analysis will form the cornerstone of the individual's continuing professional development.

Training needs analysis

The process of analysing training needs can be split into two distinctly different parts:

- the identification of the individual's current skill-set (the audit);

- the training necessary to meet the needs of the individual's priorities for the future (analysis).

Audit

Performing a training audit is the first step in the process of identifying the individual's current set of skills, the level of those skills and the resulting training needs. Information to support this process can be sourced from the following:

- training budgets;
- organisational structures;
- aims and objectives;
- strategic plans;
- job descriptions;
- training/appraisal records;
- course outlines;
- user surveys;
- questionnaires;
- interviews;
- observation.

These sources offer opportunities for the individual to gather data to develop a collective description of their skill-set, built up and maintained over a period of time. These records will stretch back over a number of years and would include details from documents relating to a first degree and any subsequent professional qualifications, not forgetting relevant work experience.

The individual should use these records to ensure that their record of training and skills is current. The emphasis here must be on continuity, to achieve any kind of consistency and to identify which skills and which training to undertake, the process must be periodically reviewed on a frequent basis.

Analysis

The following questions (amended from work by Williamson[7]) should be asked by the individual after performing an audit to analyse their needs.

- What training is needed?
- Why is it necessary?
- In what form will it be delivered?
- Where and who will provide it?

Prioritising one's needs is paramount in ensuring that training meets a real need. It is easy to attend a training session because one can, rather than because it meets a genuine need. Pinpointing the most appropriate method of learning for oneself is crucial if the training is to be effective. Possible training methods the individual might utilise include:

- case studies;
- computer-assisted learning aids (such as CD-based tutorials);
- demonstrations;
- discussions;
- e-learning (such as that provided through VLEs);
- external courses;
- focus groups;
- internal courses;

- job shadowing;
- lectures;
- observations;
- on-the-job training;
- open (or flexible) learning;
- professional reading;
- role-play;
- secondments;
- visits;
- workshops.

All of these can be utilised by the individual to acquire new skills. The effectiveness of the learning undertaken will depend on the preferred learning style of the individual and the availability of the training.

Other factors also have a bearing on the training undertaken, including support from the employing organisation, which is important and can make the difference between undertaking training or having to miss out. The time taken for a course of study or session may also be a deciding factor when arranging training for one or even for joint training sessions with colleagues. The circumstances of the individual will dictate how much and how often they can put into their professional development. They will be affected by their (or their organisation's) present or future need. This may require an immediate need for re-skilling for both the individual and the organization in some circumstances. Careful planning will lead to the improvement of skills for the individual, and as a consequence, a professional service for the employer.

Portfolios

The action of building a portfolio gathers together evidence that gives an indication of our personal level of skills. Identifying one's training needs is a time-consuming task and it requires sifting through a considerable body of documentation, both physically (printed) and virtually (electronic). To ensure that nothing is lost during this process it is vital that it is recorded. Any method of recording should track the individual's skills development in both the theoretical and practical aspects of their professional skill-set.

Portfolios should reflect the individual's achievements to date and their planned objectives, as they fulfil their professional development needs, not purely the requirements of the employer or the professional association. It is unlikely that any recording system developed through any project or professional organisation will fulfil the needs of most information professionals. This does not negate their use, but they should be used as the basis of a recording system which can be used to record skills development for the individual. However, as professionals we must expand on these to record those skills that need to be attained or developed to a higher level. Building a portfolio that includes these essentials is not an easy or small task, but individuals should not expect it to be, as it is a mechanism for ensuring continuous professional development.

What makes a portfolio?

A good portfolio requires:

- organisation;
- time;
- planning;

- structure;
- tools;
- selectivity;
- evidence.

Organisation

To be successful at creating a portfolio one has to be organised. This requires keeping copies of all relevant documents, continuously collecting and collating material.

Time

Do not underestimate the considerable amount of time it takes to organise.

Planning

Planning may be the most important aspect of creating a portfolio. If insufficient time is given over to planning the structure, then it is highly likely that considerable changes will have to be made to restructure the portfolio at a later date. This will be dictated by the style and method of working that the individual favours; creating a portfolio is a hard task, which should not be further complicated by working in a different manner.

Structure

Deciding on the appropriate structure and adopting a method to make it work is a skill in itself and will aid the professional development process. Remember that the material may fit one structure better than another and it is more important that the structure supports the evidence of the individual's own skills development.

Tools

The structure may be predetermined by the organisation with which the individual is associated, or if not they may provide a tool that can be used to help the process. It may guide them in examining their own needs and aid them in finding a structure that suits their way of working.

Selectivity

It is important that the individual is particularly selective regarding the material that they include. Only material that is relevant to the skills or criteria being addressed should be included, whatever format it may take.

Evidence

All evidence gathered by the individual to support their professional development should be:

- valid;
- reliable;
- sufficient;
- authentic;
- current;
- specific.

These checks are crucial to the successful selection of evidence for inclusion in the portfolio.

What to include in a portfolio?

When beginning to create a portfolio the emphasis should be on collecting material. As a guide the following information should be included in a portfolio:

- CV including job titles and descriptions;
- evidence on recent skills development;
- annotated contents;
- an objective, evaluative introduction (including learning style);
- aims and objectives of the employing organisation (and understanding);
- examples of commitment to CPD, including targets and goals;
- understanding of, and involvement with the professional body;
- details of relevant learning/training;
- identification of strengths and weaknesses;
- bibliography;
- listing of visits and courses.

Individuals may want to contribute additional data but this will provide a solid foundation for anyone's professional development.

Evidence

Evidence from a wide ranging series of sources should be employed, including:

- examples of work;
- journal;
- responses to enquiries from users/colleagues;
- project involvement;
- publicity created;
- photographs;

- reports (meetings, evaluations);
- letters/memoranda;
- guidance notes to staff/users;
- contributions to professional press;
- training (evaluation forms);
- personal reports (meetings, events, visits);
- case studies;
- testimonies/observations;
- multimedia.

If the evidence is to be meaningful to those viewing the portfolio then annotations must be made. Each annotation should convey the following information:

- what the evidence is;
- who created it;
- when it was created;
- why it was created;
- what the evidence shows;
- keywords.

Structure

A portfolio can be structured in a number of ways to show the professional development.

- time;
- individual pieces of work;
- topic or theme;
- learning outcome or assessment criteria.

The individual should make the ultimate decision themselves and should choose the approach that best fits their way of working.

Portfolio indexing

The portfolio must be indexed to enable a reviewer to access the information they need. Annotating the evidence is the first part of this process and including keywords on each piece will help the indexing process. If the evidence has keywords then a simple index using the keywords can be created and reference made to each piece. When creating an index one should try to bear in mind the questions that may be asked of the portfolio which might include:

- Where can I find information on this topic?
- Where can I find the feedback on this work?
- Where are the finished articles, projects etc.?

The portfolio can be used to complement existing personal and professional development tools. It can provide:

- recognition of the individual's full range of skills;
- awareness of their skills in the marketplace through reflection;
- the ability for individuals to analyse their skills and express their competencies.

Development programmes

Training and development opportunities can come in a variety of forms and at a variety of levels from membership organisations internationally, nationally, sectorally and locally.

Continuing professional development is a significant part of learning and should:

- 'maintain members technical knowledge, professional skills and competencies;
- assist them to remain flexible and adaptable; and
- provide reasonable assurance to the community that they are keeping themselves up-to-date'.[8]

Continuing professional development schemes ensure members have to achieve compliance with these standards. This is in line with other professions that insist that members keep their skills and competencies up-to-date, ensuring that both the individual and the profession have achieved a high standard of professionalism. Suitable activities for professional development can include:

- professional reading;
- formal education and training;
- informal learning activities;
- presentations and papers;
- publications;
- attendance at conferences and meetings;
- association activities;
- workplace learning.

An audited scheme proves that individuals are both professionally active and that their skills and knowledge are current. Employers who employ these professionals and then support them, are making a conscious decision to invest in their staff. The One Umbrella Report recognises this and states, 'in a fast paced employment market, those with proven, up-to-date skills are able to take advantage of the most attractive job opportunities'.[9] Members can find assistance through tools provided by professional associations, which aim to:

- help individuals analyse their development needs;
- set objectives to address these needs;
- obtain input from managers, mentors and colleagues;
- maintain an appropriate record of professional development;
- assess development needs for the future.

These schemes are new to the profession and are becoming more prevalent. This is important as there is a need to prove to employers, in an increasingly competitive market, that members of the library and information profession are eminently employable and are an asset to the employing organisation.

Organisations provide support for professionals in different spheres of the library and information profession. However, they see that it is the responsibility of the individual to 'raise the bar against which members measure their commitment to professional excellence through continued learning'.[10] They also see that professional development is a shared responsibility and a partnership between the individual, graduate schools of library and information science and the institutions that employ them. Each partner has an important role to play in professional development, but it hinges on a commitment by the individual for personal growth.

Individuals should:[11]

- identify the personal and professional skills and knowledge necessary for present and future needs;

- continuously assess their skills and knowledge;
- use the above processes to develop a personal learning strategy.

Professional bodies should provide:[12]

- help in identifying and participating in professional development programmes;
- facilitating personal approaches to learning, e.g. seminars, meetings and publications;
- assessment tools for evaluating skills and competencies;
- opportunities for collaborative learning with partners.

Library and information science schools should:

- foster this process at an early stage;
- promote the individual's own analysis of their learning styles;
- promote the concept of continuing professional development.

Employing institutions should show their commitment by:

- offering financial support;
- giving time off for study or other means.

These are important support mechanisms for members of professional bodies and for non-members. If the individual is not a member then they will be largely unaware of the majority of the activities that a professional association can, and does provide. The individual should consider membership, if not for professional qualifications, then for the support that it offers.

Professional bodies can support professional development by:

- creating mentor programmes;
- offering loans and scholarships;
- reducing rates for conferences and programmes;
- strong publications programme;
- providing means for members to talk to each other, such as online discussion groups.

The employing organisation will often have schemes that can be used to support professional development, although they may not be perceived as such. These can include:

- staff development reviews;
- appraisal schemes;
- performance reviews;
- mentoring;
- staff development schemes.

These will differ from organisation to organisation, but in general they offer the individual a means to access training specific to their needs.

Employers are aware that their most valuable asset is their staff and consequently may make resources available for developing their own personnel. This provides benefits for the individual in the form of readily accessible training and development. Many firms offer support for their staff and it is worth investigating what is available and how to access this.

Support networks

Other networking exists outside professional membership, including the following:

- personal contacts;
- colleagues;
- courses;
- discussion groups;
- weblogs;
- newsfeeds and RSS.

Courses may be made accessible in some of the following formats:

- computer-assisted learning aids (e.g. CD-based tutorials);
- e-learning (such as that provided through VLEs);
- open (or flexible) learning;
- exhibitions;
- internal courses;
- external courses;
- seminars;
- workshops;
- focus groups.

Anderson and Kanuka[13] state that online discussion groups have the following benefits for individuals:

- no limitations on time;
- ability to reflect before taking part;

- capability for research;
- communication on a global scale.

Subtle differences exist between online forums. According to Bernier and Bowen[14] the different forums are:

- bulletin board systems;
- mailing lists;
- newsgroups;
- web forums.

Users can join in with online groups whenever they feel it is appropriate and can reflect on their contribution before they make themselves known to the online forum. It enables individuals across the globe to discuss issues with those in locations remote from their own workplace.

Mentoring

Traditionally the relationship between master and apprentice was the mentoring process at its most productive. The experienced master would train and develop the skills of the apprentice so that skills would be transferred to future generations. Mentoring has changed considerably over the years, but the concept still remains the same. Mentoring will normally include these phases:[15]

- initiation;
- goal setting;
- developmental learning;
- winding down;
- dissolving.

The mentor will lead the individual through these phases and should incorporate different methods to help the individual into the relationship. Clutterbuck[16] suggests five styles to support the development of the individual.

- coaching;
- counselling;
- networking;
- guiding;
- mentoring.

The individual will be able to judge the ability of their mentor by recognising these styles and should also look for some of the following qualities in their mentor. They should be:

- 'good motivators, perceptive, able to support the objectives of the programme and fulfil their responsibilities to the candidate;
- high performers, secure in their own position within the organisation and unlikely to feel threatened by, or resentful of, the candidate's opportunities;
- able to show that a responsibility for mentoring is part of their own job description;
- able to establish a good and professional relationship, be sympathetic, accessible and knowledgeable about the candidate's area of interest;
- sufficiently senior to be in touch with the corporate structure, sharing the company's values and able to give the candidate access to resources and information;
- good teachers, able to advise and instruct without interfering, allowing candidates to explore and pursue ideas even though they may not be optimum pathways;

- good negotiators, willing and able to plan alongside their own management teams and academics'.[17]

It is not only mentors that must possess the appropriate qualities for mentoring. Mentees must also exhibit the following qualities to get the best from the experience:

- personal ambition;
- wish to be mentored;
- context to their work;
- building of confidence;
- willingness to learn;
- clear goals;
- ability to analyse and reflect on their experience;
- plan their career;
- need to develop personally;
- need to develop professionally.

The mentoring process, like many, is iterative. It begins with an analysis of the situation followed by an identification of the options available and the selection of the appropriate action. After implementing this, both the mentee and the mentor will review progress before deciding whether the action achieved its purpose or whether an alternative course should be taken. Finally this should be reflected upon and evaluated before re-starting the process.

Benefits for all through mentoring

The process of mentoring brings benefits to all those involved. According to The National Library Board[18] they include, for the mentee:

- advice on career planning, personal and professional development;
- acquisition of new skills;
- understanding about career development;
- widening of networking circle;
- support in managing change and difficulties;
- boost to self-esteem;
- encouragement to take up new projects and responsibilities;
- insight into organisational policies;
- enhanced management skills;
- reduced professional isolation.

Benefits are not limited to the mentee; both the mentor and line manager will receive the following benefits:[19]

- personal satisfaction;
- development of professional skills, such as counselling;
- incentive to keep abreast of professional developments;
- exposure to new ideas and different perspectives of the profession;
- widening of professional network;
- career enhancement;
- giving something back to profession.

The organisation and the profession also benefit from the mentoring process through:

- increased productivity;
- improvement in managers' skills;
- more flexible organisation;

- staff empowerment;
- increased commitment from new and experienced staff;
- increased understanding of organisations goals;
- lower staff turnover;
- less staff burnout;
- enhanced learning culture;
- leadership and successor planning.[20]

Mentoring schemes are not widely known in the library and information sector, however many professionals give up their time to help individuals. If the opportunity to benefit from a scheme becomes available then it should be taken.

Financing development

Courses may be too expensive for the individual to fund. However, they may be able to obtain funding from other sources, including:

- the employer;
- event organisers;
- professional associations and groups;
- educational establishments.

Continuing professional development is essential for the library and information worker to ensure that their skills and competencies remain current. This will maintain the reputation of the professional and the service that they are providing to the users. Most information professionals will see this as their reason for continually renewing and developing their skill-set. However, the individual should not see this as their only reason for building upon previous development, it is entirely valid to use the process as a vehicle for progressing one's career.

Career planning

Emphasis should also be placed on the individual's career development. Some individuals may prefer to plan ahead for a particular role, while others may wish to take advantage of opportunities as they arise. Evans, Layzell Ward and Rugaas[21] state that the following should be considered when making a personal assessment of one's skills to plan for any future career:

- level of qualifications;
- short courses attended;
- study currently being undertaken;
- professional activities;
- committee work within the organisation;
- work experience;
- preferred career direction;
- preferred sector;
- preferred specialisation;
- areas currently not under consideration by the individual;
- personal strengths;
- personal weaknesses;
- commitment to librarianship and information work in the long term;
- external factors that are personally important and may restrict professional growth.

Career planning is essential if one is to keep on track for their original career goal; planning, like professional development should be a continuous process. The continuously evolving library and information environment will present increasing opportunities for the committed professional; it is therefore essential to plan and keep a record of that plan.

Setting career goals

Today career patterns are much more flexible and one may change employer and even sector on a frequent basis. However, the factors that lead to the successful progression in one's career are consistent. The individual should focus their attention on their:

- qualifications;
- experience;
- attitude;
- aptitude.

Prospective employers will have these attributes in mind when reviewing applications and when interviewing candidates. They will be assessing whether the individual's qualifications match those required and whether that same individual has the required experience for the post. Both attitude and aptitude of the individual will be judged on one's application and the further stages of the application process. Career development depends on continuous professional development. Individuals will need to:

- analyse their professional development needs;
- set their own objectives to meet these needs;
- use mentors and line managers as sounding boards;

- create a method for storing this knowledge;
- prioritise activities and plans for the future.

Conclusion

As a final checklist, the authors Evans, Layzell Ward and Rugaas[22] developed a checklist for the factors that contribute to career success. Many of these apply to continuing professional development and if borne in mind can lead to satisfaction in one's chosen career.

- Know one's strengths and weaknesses.
- Demonstrate high standards personally and professionally.
- Be committed.
- Be reliable.
- Be objective and think clearly.
- Be able to support others both personally and professionally.
- Keep up-to-date with changes in the profession and sector.
- Be an effective team member.
- Manage one's time effectively.
- Recognise one's mistakes and triumphs, reflect and learn from them.

Bear these in mind and plan accordingly to develop oneself both personally and professionally for a better career, not forgetting that life requires balance in all things both personal and professional.

Notes

1. D. Kolb. *Continuing Professional Development: http://www1 .bcs.org.uk/bm.asp?sectionID=1047* (visited 20 March 2004).
2. D.A. Schon (1982) *The Reflective Practitioner.* New York: Basic Books.
3. Ibid.
4. J. Cowan (1998) *On Becoming an Innovative University Teacher: Reflection in Action.* Buckingham: Society for Research into Higher Education and Open University Press.
5. P. Honey and A. Mumford (1986) *Using your Learning Styles.* Maidenhead: Peter Honey.
6. T. Boydell and M. Leary (1996) *Identifying Training Needs.* London: Institute of Personnel and Development.
7. M. Williamson (1993) *Training Needs Analysis.* London: Library Association Publishing.
8. Australian Library and Information Association. *Continuing Professional Development: http://www.alia.org.au/education/ cpd/index.html* (visited 27 January 2004).
9. The One Umbrella Team (2001). Continuing Professional Development update. *TOUR: The One Umbrella Report,* 2(1): *http://www.oneumbrella.com.au* (visited 15 March 2004).
10. Association of College and Research Libraries. *ACRL Statement on Staff Development: http://www.ala.org/ala/acrl/ acrlpubs/whitepapers/acrlstatement.htm* (visited 23 March 2004).
11. Ibid.
12. Ibid.
13. T. Anderson and H. Kanuka (1997) On-line Forums: New Platforms for Professional Development and Group Collaboration. *Journal of Computer-mediated Communication,* 3:*http://www.ascusc.org/jcmc/vol3/issue3/anderson.html* (visited 17 September 2004).
14. R. Bernier and J.P. Bowen (2004) Web-based Discussion Groups at Stake: the Profile of Museum Professionals Online. *Program: Electronic Library and Information Systems,* 38: 120–137.

15. University of Hull, Business School. *The Empathy Project E-mentoring Guidelines*: *http://www.hull.ac.uk/hubs/empathy/documents/Mentoring%20Guidance%20for%203rd%20Year%20HUBS%20Students.doc* (visited 20 April 2004).

16. D. Clutterbuck (2001) *Everyone Needs a Mentor: Fostering Talent at Work*. 3rd edn. London: Chartered Institute of Personnel and Development; pp. 19–21.

17. E. Parsloe (1995) *The Manager as Coach and Mentor*. London: Institute of Personnel and Development; pp. 25–26.

18. The National Library Board. *Mentoring: Information Services Topical Brief*: *http://www.consal.org.sg/webupload/resource/brief/attachments/%7B6FFF607C-3A70-4D43-884E-B10A4FE70B45%7D.pdf* (visited 17 September 2004).

19. Ibid.

20. Ibid.

21. G.E. Evans, P. Layzell Ward and B. Rugaas. *Career Development* (Chapter 20): *http://www.neal-schuman.com/career.htm* (visited 1 July 2004).

22. Ibid.

Index

Terms used very often throughout this text such as professional development have not been included in this index.

Printed in the United Kingdom
by Lightning Source UK Ltd.
109980UKS00001B/54